CONGREGATION FOR THE CLERGY

THE GIFT OF THE PRIESTLY VOCATION

Ratio Fundamentalis
Institutionis Sacerdotalis

*All documents are published thanks to the generous support
of the members of the Catholic Truth Society*

CATHOLIC TRUTH SOCIETY
PUBLISHERS TO THE HOLY SEE

First published 2017 by The Incorporated Catholic Truth Society 40-46 Harleyford Road London SE11 5AY Tel: 020 7640 0042 Fax: 020 7640 0046. Copyright © 2017 Libreria Editrice Vaticana, Cittá del Vaticano.

ISBN 978 1 78469 181 3

CONTENTS

INTRODUCTION... 5
1. The need for a new *Ratio Fundamentalis Institutionis Sacerdotalis*..... 5
2. Preparatory Stages.. 6
3. Characteristic Elements and Fundamental Content 7

I. GENERAL NORMS [1-10] 11
(a) Sphere of Application 11
(b) Preparation of the *Ratio Nationalis* 13
(c) Responsibilities of the Conferences of Bishops................... 14
(d) National and International Seminary Organisations.............. 15
(e) The Programme of Formation for each Seminary 16

II. PRIESTLY VOCATIONS [11-27]................................ 17
(a) General Principles 17
(b) Minor Seminaries and Other Forms
    of Accompaniment for Adolescents 19
(c) Mature Vocations.. 22
(d) Vocations Arising among Indigenous Peoples................... 23
(e) Vocations and Migrants.. 23

III. THE FOUNDATIONS OF FORMATION [28-53] 25
(a) The Subject of Formation 25
(b) The Basis and the Purpose of Formation: Priestly Identity......... 26
(c) The Journey of Formation as Configuration to Christ............. 28
(d) A Formation for Interior Life and Communion 30
(e) Means of Formation... 33
    e.1. Personal Accompaniment 33
    e.2. Community Accompaniment.............................. 35
(f) The Unity of Formation 36

IV. INITIAL AND ONGOING FORMATION [54-88] 37
(a) Initial Formation and its Stages................................ 38
    a.1. The Propaedeutic Stage................................... 39
    a.2. The Stage of Philosophical studies (or Discipleship) 40
    a.3. The Stage of Theological Studies (or Configuration) 42
    a.4. The Pastoral Stage (or Vocational Synthesis) 45
(b) Ongoing Formation 47

3

V. Dimensions of Formation [89-124] 54
(a) Integrating the Dimensions of Formation 54
(b) The Human Dimension 56
(c) The Spiritual Dimension 60
(d) The Intellectual Dimension 67
(e) The Pastoral Dimension 68

VI. The Agents of Formation [125-152] 73
(a) The Diocesan Bishop 74
(b) The Presbyterate 75
(c) The Seminarians 75
(d) The Community of Formators 76
(e) The Professors 79
(f) Specialists 81
(g) The Family, the Parish and Other Ecclesial Communities 81
(h) Consecrated Life and Laity in Formation 82
(i) Ongoing Formation for all Agents of Formation 83

VII. The Organisation of Studies [153-187] 84
(a) The Study of Propaedeutic Materials 85
(b) Philosophical Studies 86
(c) Theological Studies 88
(d) "Ministerial" Subjects 94
(e) Specialised Studies 97
(f) The Goals and Methods of Teaching 98

VIII. Criteria and Norms [188-209] 100
(a) Various Forms of Seminary 100
(b) Admission, Dismissal and Departure from the Seminary 101
    b.1. Physical Health 101
    b.2. Psychological Health 102
    b.3. Dismissal 105
    b.4. Seminarians Coming from Other Seminaries
    or Institutes of Formation 105
(c) Persons with Homosexual Tendencies 106
(d) The Protection of Minors and the Accompaniment of Victims 107
(e) The Scrutinies 108
    Conclusion 112

INTRODUCTION

1. THE NEED FOR A NEW RATIO FUNDAMENTALIS INSTITUTIONIS SACERDOTALIS

The gift of the priestly vocation, placed by God in the hearts of some men, obliges the Church to propose to them a serious journey of formation. As Pope Francis recalled on the occasion of his address to the Plenary of the Congregation for the Clergy (3 October 2014): "It means guarding and fostering vocations, that they may bear mature fruit. They are 'uncut diamonds', to be formed both patiently and carefully, respecting the conscience of the individual, so that they may shine among the People of God".[1]

It was some thirty years ago - on 19 March 1985 - that the Congregation for Catholic Education, then competent in this matter, proceeded to amend the *Ratio Fundamentalis Institutionis Sacerdotalis* promulgated on 6 January 1970[2], above all by updating the footnotes in light of the promulgation of the *Code of Canon Law* (25 January 1983).

Since then there have been numerous contributions on the theme of the formation of future priests, both on the part of the Universal Church and on the part of the Conferences of Bishops and individual particular Churches.

It is necessary above all to recall the Magisterium of the Pontiffs who have guided the Church in this time: St John Paul II, to whom we owe the ground-breaking Post-Synodal Apostolic Exhortation *Pastores Dabo Vobis* (25 March 1992); Benedict XVI, author of the Apostolic Letter motu proprio *Ministrorum Institutio* (16 January 2013); and Francis, whose encouragement and suggestions gave rise to the present document.

Pastores Dabo Vobis, in particular, explicitly sets out an integrated vision of the formation of future clerics, taking equal account of all four dimensions that involve the person of the seminarian: human, intellectual, spiritual and pastoral. *Ministrorum Institutio* seeks to show how the

---

[1] FRANCIS, Address to the Plenary of the Congregation for Clergy (3 October 2014): *L'Osservatore Romano*, 226 (4 October 2014), 8.

[2] Cf. CONGREGATION FOR CATHOLIC EDUCATION, *Ratio Fundamentalis Institutionis Sacerdotalis* (6 January 1970): AAS 62 (1970), 321-384.

formation of seminarians finds a natural continuation in the ongoing formation of priests, so that the two form one single reality. For this reason, Benedict XVI decided to entrust responsibility for initial formation in the seminary to the Congregation for the Clergy, which was already competent for the ongoing formation of clergy. He amended, therefore, the relevant articles of the Apostolic Constitution *Pastor Bonus* (28 June 1988), and transferred the Office for Seminaries to the Congregation for the Clergy. During his pontificate, Pope Francis has offered a rich Magisterium and a constant personal example regarding the ministry and life of priests, encouraging and supporting the work that has led to this present document.

In these years there have been plenty of documents issued by dicasteries of the Roman Curia, regarding particular aspects of the formation of future priests - the Congregation for Catholic Education, the Congregation for Divine Worship and the Discipline of the Sacraments, as well as the Congregation for the Clergy - not to mention the various national formation programmes, many of which have been consulted in the course of this work.[3]

2. PREPARATORY STAGES

The Congregation for the Clergy began preparing the first draft of the present *Ratio Fundamentalis* in the spring of 2014. It was sent to some experts and, in particular, to the members of the dicastery, in preparation for the Plenary Assembly of the Congregation, which took place from 1 to 3 October 2014. During that Plenary, the text was discussed and commented upon by the Cardinal and bishop members, and by the invited experts, who offered proposals and suggestions for the progress of the work.

This material was used to draw up a fuller text, enriched by the suggestions received from a number of dicasteries of the Roman Curia, both those with an interest in the question by virtue of their competence (the Congregation for the Evangelisation of Peoples, the Congregation for Institutes of Consecrated Life and Societies of Apostolic Life, and the Congregation for the Oriental Churches), and those with a previously acquired experience in the field (the Congregation for Catholic Education).

---

[3] These documents will be mentioned in detail, and taken into account in a specific way, in the text which follows.

Introduction

During 2015, the text was sent to numerous Conferences of Bishops and Apostolic Nunciatures, in order to seek their opinion and to broaden the scope of the consultation and reflection, so as to include countries in which the *Ratio Fundamentalis* will be applied, in the spirit of synodality that is so frequently highlighted by Pope Francis.

The Congregation for the Clergy also organised an International Conference, held on 19 and 20 November 2015, to mark the 50th anniversary of the conciliar documents *Optatam Totius* and *Presbyterorum Ordinis*, during which Cardinals, bishops, professors, formators and experts offered their own valuable contributions to the discussion of the formation of candidates for Holy Orders.

The Congregation for the Clergy, taking into due consideration the contributions received, then prepared a definitive draft. This was examined firstly by some consultors, and was then presented to a number of dicasteries of the Roman Curia (the Secretariat of State, the Congregation for the Doctrine of the Faith, the Congregation for Divine Worship and the Discipline of the Sacraments, the Congregation for Bishops, the Congregation for the Evangelisation of Peoples, the Congregation for Institutes of Consecrated Life and Societies of Apostolic Life, the Congregation for Catholic Education, the Congregation for the Causes of Saints, the Congregation for the Oriental Churches, the Pontifical Council for Legislative Texts), in accordance with the spirit of co-responsibility and cooperation that is encouraged by Article 17 of the Apostolic Constitution *Pastor Bonus*.

At the end of this process of consultation and in light of the suggestions received, a definitive text was drafted, to be placed before Pope Francis for his approval, according to Article 18 of *Pastor Bonus*.

3. CHARACTERISTIC ELEMENTS AND FUNDAMENTAL CONTENT

The journey of priestly formation, beginning with the seminary years, is described in the present *Ratio Fundamentalis* in terms of four characteristic elements of formation, understood as one, integral, grounded in community and missionary in spirit.

The formation of priests means following a singular "journey of discipleship", which begins at Baptism, is perfected through the other sacraments of Christian initiation, comes to be appreciated as the centre of one's life at the beginning of seminary formation, and continues through the whole of life.

Formation - both initial and ongoing - must be seen through a unifying lens, which takes account of the four dimensions of formation proposed by *Pastores Dabo Vobis*. Together, these dimensions give shape and structure to the identity of the seminarian and the priest, and make him capable of that "gift of self to the Church", which is the essence of pastoral charity. The entire journey of formation must never be reduced to a single aspect to the detriment of others, but it must always be an integrated journey of the disciple called to priesthood.

This formation has an eminently communitarian character from the outset. In fact, the vocation to the priesthood is a gift that God gives to the Church and to the world, a path to sanctify oneself and others that should not be followed in an individualistic manner, but must always have as its point of reference a specific portion of the People of God. Such a vocation is discovered and accepted within a community. It is formed in the seminary, in the context of an educating community, comprised of various members of the People of God. This community leads the seminarian, through ordination, to become part of the "family" of the presbyterate, at the service of a particular community. With respect to the priest formators, this *Ratio Fundamentalis* wishes to emphasise that, for the effectiveness of their endeavours, they must consider themselves to be a true formative community. They should act accordingly, sharing a common responsibility, with due regard to the duties and the office entrusted to each member.

Since the priest-disciple comes from the Christian community, and will be sent back to it, to serve it and to guide it as a pastor, formation is clearly missionary in character. Its goal is participation in the one mission entrusted by Christ to his Church, that is evangelisation, in all its forms.

The fundamental idea is that seminaries should form missionary disciples who are "in love" with the Master, shepherds "with the smell of the sheep", who live in their midst to bring the mercy of God to them. Hence every priest should always feel that he is a disciple on a journey, constantly needing an integrated formation, understood as a continuous configuration to Christ.

Within this single integrated and continuous formation, two phases can be identified, namely initial and ongoing. In this *Ratio Fundamentalis*, initial formation is divided into various stages: the propaedeutic stage, the study of philosophy or the discipleship stage; the study of theology or the configurative stage, and the pastoral stage or that of vocational synthesis.

Seen in these terms, the journey of formation has developed in several ways since the *Ratio Fundamentalis* of 1970. Following the experimentation and trial period, begun by the Synod of Bishops of 1990 (VIII General Assembly), the "propaedeutic stage", with its specific identity and formative purpose, is now presented as necessary and mandatory.

As regards the "discipleship" and "configuration" stages, these terms are placed alongside the customary periods of "philosophical studies" and "theological studies", which are intended to last for six years altogether.[4] Moreover, it should be emphasised that the intellectual dimension, with the prescribed study of philosophy and theology, is not the only factor to be considered when evaluating the journey completed by the seminarian in each stage, and the progress that has been made. Rather the overall discernment by the formators regarding all the aspects of formation will allow only those seminarians to pass on to the next stage who, in addition to having passed the necessary exams, have reached the level of human and vocational maturity required for each stage.

Finally, the "pastoral stage", or the "stage of vocational synthesis", is intended to give particular importance to the period between the end of formation in the seminary and priestly ordination, with the purpose of helping the candidate to acquire the necessary understanding in preparation for it.

Discipleship and configuration to Christ, obviously, last throughout life. The terms "discipleship stage" and "configuration stage" are intended to focus attention on two moments of initial formation, on the special attention to be given to the awareness of being disciples, and on the need to understand the call to ministry and priestly life as a continuous configuration to Christ.

As for ongoing formation, by its nature this cannot be set out in ready made "stages". For this reason, only certain moments, situations and

---

[4] Cf. C.I.C., can. 250.

tools have been mentioned. These may be of help to priests and to those engaged in the task of ongoing formation, so as to experience and to offer concrete initiatives.

A further integral part of this *Ratio Fundamentalis*, as of the 1970 edition, is the *Ordo Studiorum*. This provides a descriptive list of materials that must be included in the course of studies for seminarians, during the various phases, within the wider intellectual formation. It must be applied in its entirety in seminaries and in those houses of formation that offer the prescribed six years of philosophy and theology courses internally. Such houses of formation, naturally, will also offer the courses of the propaedeutic stage and those which pertain specifically to ministry.

Guidelines of various kinds - theological, spiritual, pedagogical, canonical - are offered in the text of this *Ratio Fundamentalis,* along with actual norms, which mirror those of the *Code of Canon Law*, and determine more precisely the manner of their application.[5] Guidelines and norms have not been rigidly separated in the document, though the mandatory or advisory nature of each passage has been made clear. Instead these two elements have been integrated into the document, in order to provide a text enriched by considerations and perspectives of various kinds.

---

[5] Cf. *ibid.*, can. 31, § 1.

I. GENERAL NORMS

(A) SPHERE OF APPLICATION

1. This *Ratio Fundamentalis Institutionis Sacerdotalis*[6] is to be applied in its entirety in those countries which fall within the competence of the Congregation for the Clergy. Taking into account, however, the Conciliar decree *Ad Gentes*, n. 16, and Article 88 §2 of the Apostolic Constitution *Pastor Bonus*, it applies in part to those territories within the competence of the Congregation for the Evangelisation of Peoples. In fact, although that dicastery has the duty "to form the secular clergy", according to its own guidelines and norms, this *Ratio* is normative as regards the "General Plan of Studies" also for those countries under the competence of the Congregation for the Evangelisation of Peoples. Moreover, the *Rationes* of the following entities must be conformed to the *Ratio Fundamentalis*, with the necessary adaptations: Institutes of Consecrated Life and Societies of Apostolic Life[7], dependent on the Congregation for Institutes of Consecrated Life and Societies of Apostolic Life, on the Congregation for the Evangelisation of Peoples, as well as on the Pontifical Commission *Ecclesia Dei*, insofar as it pertains to "*members who are being prepared for sacred orders*"[8]; Clerical Associations who have been granted the right to incardinate clerics; Personal Prelatures; Military Ordinariates; and Personal Ordinariates.[9] For this reason, when reference is made to competences of the Ordinary, this includes Major Superiors of Clerical Institutes of Consecrated Life and Societies of Apostolic Life of pontifical right, unless it is clear from the context that only the diocesan bishop is intended.

---

[6] The document is a general executory decree, *ex* can. 31, § 1 C.I.C., which, in applying the canonical norms regarding formation, replaces the *Ratio Fundamentalis Institutionis Sacerdotalis* of 6 January 1970, and its revised edition of 19 March 1985; cf. Second Vatican Ecumenical Council, Decree on the Formation of Priests, *Optatam Totius* (28 October 1965), n. 1: *AAS* 58 (1966), 713.

[7] Cf. JOHN PAUL II, Apostolic Constitution *Pastor Bonus* (28 June 1988), articles 88, § 2 and 108, § 2: *AAS* 80 (1988), 882 and 887.

[8] C.I.C., can. 659, § 3.

[9] Cf. BENEDICT XVI, Apostolic Constitution *Anglicanorum Coetibus* (4 November 2009): *AAS* 101 (2009), 985-990.

In accordance with the norms of Articles 56 and 58 §2 of the Apostolic Constitution *Pastor Bonus*, this *Ratio Fundamentalis* does not apply to the Eastern Catholic Churches subject to the competence of the Congregation for the Oriental Churches. They must prepare their own norms on this subject, based on their own liturgical, theological, spiritual and disciplinary patrimony.

It should be noted that in houses of formation of movements and of new ecclesial communities, this *Ratio Fundamentalis*, along with the *Ratio Nationalis* prepared by the Conference of Bishops of the country in which the institute is found, is to be applied in its entirety, under the authority of the diocesan bishop. Regarding the academic study of philosophy and theology, as defined in canonical, ecclesiastical or civil legislation, and regarding ecclesiastical faculties, the Congregation for Catholic Education is competent.[10] Furthermore the same Congregation is responsible for maintaining accords with the competent civil authorities.

2. The Congregation for the Clergy, which is responsible for the Pontifical Work for Priestly Vocations[11], "*gives practical expression to the concern of the Apostolic See for the formation of those called to Holy Orders*" and, among its institutional competencies, is to assist "*bishops in ensuring that in their Churches vocations to the sacred ministries are fostered with all possible diligence and that students are suitably educated in seminaries and provided with a sound human, spiritual, doctrinal and pastoral formation*".[12]

In this way, the Congregation for the Clergy promotes the pastoral care of vocations, especially vocations to Holy Orders, and offers bishops and Conferences of Bishops principles and norms for the initial and ongoing formation of clerics.

---

[10] The respective competencies of the two dicasteries were established by Benedict XVI, Apostolic Letter motu proprio *Ministrorum Institutio* (16 January 2013), art. 6: *AAS* 105 (2013), 134: "*The Congregation for Catholic Education is competent to structure the academic curricula of philosophy and theology, after consultation with the Congregation for the Clergy in areas of its respective competence*".

[11] Cf. Pius XII, motu proprio *Cum Nobis* (4 November 1941), n. 13: *AAS* 33 (1941), 479; *Ministrorum Institutio*, art. 7: *AAS* 105 (2013), 134.

[12] *Ministrorum Institutio*, articles 4-5: *AAS* 105 (2013), 133-134, which modified articles 93, § 2 and 94 of the Apostolic Constitution *Pastor Bonus*.

(B) PREPARATION OF THE RATIO NATIONALIS

3. Each Conference of Bishops is required to prepare its own *Ratio Nationalis* on the basis of this *Ratio Fundamentalis Institutionis Sacerdotalis*, which, in accordance with no. 1 of the Conciliar Decree *Optatam Totius* and can. 242 §1 of the *Code of Canon Law*, must be approved by this same Congregation, after having heard the opinion of the Congregation for Catholic Education on matters within its competence. This is to ensure the necessary harmonisation and coordination of the Programme of Studies and its consistency with the Programme of Studies of individual countries.

Whenever it may prove necessary to make changes to a previously approved *Ratio Nationalis*, due to new or unexpected developments, the text may be amended by seeking the further approval of the Congregation for the Clergy. The *Ratio Nationalis* will require revision by the competent committee of the Conference of Bishops on the basis of accumulated experience, or upon the expiry of a fixed term, and should be submitted once again for the approval of this dicastery. Further revisions and the necessary approvals can and must be undertaken and requested periodically, whenever it seems necessary to the Conference of Bishops or when, for a just cause, the Congregation for the Clergy considers it opportune.[13]

4. The right and duty to prepare the *Ratio Nationalis Institutionis Sacerdotalis*, as well as that of approving particular developments within the territory of the Conference of Bishops or the region, if it is opportune and useful to do so, belongs to Conferences of Bishops and not to individual bishops.[14]

The norms of such a *Ratio* must be observed in all diocesan and interdiocesan seminaries in the country[15] while their particular application must be given effect in the Statutes, the Rule of Life and the Programme of Formation of each institution.[16]

---

[13] Cf. C.I.C., can. 242, § 1.
[14] Cf. *ibid.*
[15] Cf. *ibid.*, can. 242, § 2.
[16] Cf. *ibid.*, can. 243.

5. In order to foster a constant dialogue between the Holy See and the particular Churches, as a sign of closeness and in order to receive advice and support, interdiocesan seminaries, in accordance with what has been established in their statutes, shall periodically send a report on their formation activities to the Congregation for the Clergy.

(C) RESPONSIBILITIES OF THE CONFERENCES OF BISHOPS

6. While safeguarding the authority of the diocesan bishop, the *Ratio Nationalis* seeks to harmonise priestly formation across the country, in this way facilitating dialogue between bishops and formators, to the benefit of both seminarians and the seminaries.[17]

7. The *Ratio Nationalis* must make reference to the dimensions of formation of candidates for the priesthood presented in this document, in such a way that the candidates can be integrally formed and properly prepared for the challenges of our time. Each *Ratio Nationalis* must also specify the stages of formation and the programme of studies, their objectives and their length, respecting the norms of universal law. In its vision of education for the priesthood, the *Ratio Nationalis* must ensure the necessary harmonisation across the whole country, while also bearing in mind any cultural diversity that may exist.

Each *Ratio Nationalis* must, in its own context, express and give effect to what is envisaged in the *Ratio Fundamentalis*, and should always include the following elements:

a. at least a summary description of the particular social, cultural and ecclesial context, in which the future priests will find themselves exercising their ministry;

b. a summary of any agreements that may have been reached by the Conference of Bishops concerning the organisation of seminaries in its country;

c. some references to the pastoral care of vocations and the means available;

d. a description of the stages of formation, placed in the context of the particular situation of the country;

---

[17] Cf. *ibid.*, can. 242, § 2.

e. a description of the means to be adopted to provide for the dimensions of formation (human, spiritual, intellectual and pastoral);

f. the programme of propaedeutic, philosophical and theological studies, including a presentation of the subjects, with some indication of the objectives and content of each, along with the number of credits required for each discipline.

8. In preparing the *Ratio Nationalis*, each Conference of Bishops should take into due consideration the characteristics and specific demands of its own socio-educational environment. Moreover, cooperation between the different ecclesiastical circumscriptions in the territory should be encouraged, paying attention to local circumstances, in order to guarantee the best programme of formation possible, as much in the larger seminaries as in the smaller ones.

According to the prudent judgement of each Conference of Bishops, the *iter* of the drafting and subsequent revisions of the *Ratio Nationalis* could involve a process of consultation. First of all, the Conference of Bishops, by means of persons duly appointed to the task, could consult the seminaries directly and, where it exists, also the national organisation for seminaries. The Conference could then entrust the preparation of a base text to the Episcopal Commission for Clergy and Seminaries. Finally, in a spirit of collegiality and cooperation, the Conference of Bishops must proceed to the final drafting of the text.

(D) NATIONAL AND INTERNATIONAL SEMINARY ORGANISATIONS

9. The establishment of supra-diocesan seminary organisations is encouraged whenever circumstances make this possible, or where similar initiatives are already underway. In fact, entities of this kind can provide valuable assistance, insofar as they can be a consultative means of communication and cooperation between formators working in different institutions. They can promote the analysis and homogenous development of educational and didactic experiences at the regional level, or a greater exchange and comparison at the international level.

The members of organisations of this kind will be drawn from the formators of the different institutions. It will be important that these organisations operate under the guidance of the Commission for Clergy and Seminaries of the Conference of Bishops. In any case, in a spirit of ecclesial communion, it is the responsibility of the Congregation for the Clergy to erect such organisations on a universal level. It belongs, however, to the Conferences of Bishops or to the various organisations of the same (for example, the Consejo Episcopal Latinoamericano [CELAM], the Consilium Conferentiarium Episcoporum Europae [CCEE], the Federation of Asian Bishops' Conferences [FABC], etc.), having consulted this Dicastery, to set up organisations operative within their territories or their continent, approving their statutes while respecting the competences of individual diocesan bishops and Conferences of Bishops.

As already happens in some regions, it could be of great help were such organisations to promote, within the territory of their competence, courses for formators and opportunities for the study of themes linked to vocations and to priestly formation. The results of these initiatives may then be made available to the relevant Conferences of Bishops.[18]

(E) THE PROGRAMME OF FORMATION FOR EACH SEMINARY

10. The diocesan bishop (or, in the case of an interdiocesan seminary, the bishops concerned), assisted by the community of formators of the seminary, has the task of developing a programme of "integrated formation", also called the formation itinerary, and of promoting its practical application[19], in a way that respects the different stages and the pedagogical journey set out therein. Taking the *Ratio Fundamentalis* as its point of reference, this programme of formation aims to apply the norms of the *Ratio Nationalis* and the pedagogical vision that inspires it, according to the circumstances and needs of the particular Church, taking into account the cultural background of the seminarians, the pastoral reality of the Diocese and its "tradition of formation".

---

[18] Cf. *Optatam Totius*, n. 5: *AAS* 58 (1966), 716-717.
[19] Cf. CONGREGATION FOR BISHOPS, Directory for the Pastoral Ministry of Bishops *Apostolorum Successores* (22 February 2004), n. 90: *Enchiridion Vaticanum* 22 (2006), 1768-1769.

II. PRIESTLY VOCATIONS

(A) GENERAL PRINCIPLES

11. Ecclesial vocations are manifestations of the immeasurable riches of Christ (cf. *Eph* 3:8). For this reason they are to be held in the highest esteem and cultivated with all diligence and concern, so that they can blossom and mature. Among the many vocations that the Holy Spirit never ceases to call forth in the People of God, the vocation to the ministerial priesthood calls one to "*participate in the hierarchical priesthood of Christ*"[20] and to be united with him "*to feed the Church in Christ's name with the word and the grace of God.*"[21] This vocation arises in various circumstances and at different stages of human life: in adolescence, in adulthood, and, as the constant experience of the Church never fails to show, also in childhood.

12. The vocation to the ministerial priesthood occurs within the wider realm of the baptismal vocation of the Christian, through which the People of God, "*established by Christ as a communion of life, charity and truth, [...] is also used by him as an instrument for the redemption of all, and is sent forth into the whole world as the light of the world and the salt of the earth* (cf. *Mt* 5:13-16)".[22]

13. It is the mission of the Church "*to care for the birth, discernment and fostering of vocations, particularly those to the priesthood*".[23] Welcoming the voice of Christ, who asks all of us to pray the Lord of the harvest to send labourers into his harvest (cf. *Mt* 9:38; *Lk* 10:2), the Church dedicates particular attention to vocations to the consecrated life and to the priesthood.

---

[20] *Optatam Totius*, n. 2: *AAS* 58 (1966), 714-715.

[21] SECOND VATICAN ECUMENICAL COUNCIL, Dogmatic Constitution on the Church *Lumen Gentium* (21 November 1964), n. 11: *AAS* 57 (1965), 15.

[22] Ibid., n. 9: *AAS* 57 (1965), 13.

[23] John Paul II, Post-Synodal Apostolic Exhortation *Pastores Dabo Vobis*, n. 34: *AAS* 84 (1992), 713.

Thus it is necessary that Vocations Offices[24] be established and promoted in dioceses, regions and countries. In collaboration with the Pontifical Work for Priestly Vocations, they are called to promote and direct the whole pastoral care of vocations[25], providing the necessary resources.[26] Bishops, first among those responsible for vocations to the priesthood, should encourage active cooperation among priests, consecrated persons and the laity (especially parents and teachers). Cooperation should also be promoted with groups, movements and associations of the lay faithful within an organic overall pastoral plan.[27]

14. Support should be given to initiatives that can encourage the gift of new vocations that come from God, above all personal and communal prayer. Certain times of the liturgical year seem particularly suited to this purpose, and it is for the competent ecclesiastical authority to establish dates for liturgical celebrations of particular significance. Some years ago the Supreme Pontiff set aside the Fourth Sunday of Easter, known as Good Shepherd Sunday, for the celebration of the annual World Day of Prayer for Vocations. It can also be helpful to support activities aimed at creating a spiritual

---

[24] Cf. CONGREGATION FOR CATHOLIC EDUCATION - PONTIFICAL WORK FOR PRIESTLY VOCATIONS, *Pastoral Guidelines for the Promotion of Vocations to the Priestly Ministry* (25 March 2012), n. 13.

[25] Cf. PONTIFICAL WORK FOR PRIESTLY VOCATIONS, *Developments in the Pastoral Care for Vocations in the Particular Churches* (6 January 1992); *Pastoral Guidelines for the Promotion of Vocations to the Priestly Ministry*.

[26] Cf. *Optatam Totius*, n. 2: *AAS* 58 (1966), 714-715; SECOND VATICAN ECUMENICAL COUNCIL, Decree on the Ministry and Life of Priests *Presbyterorum Ordinis* (7 December 1965), n. 11: *AAS* 58 (1966), 1008-1009; Decree on the Renewal of Religious Life *Perfectae Caritatis* (28 October 1965), n. 24: *AAS* 58 (1966), 711-712; Decree on the Pastoral Office of Bishops in the Church *Christus Dominus* (28 October 1965), n. 15: *AAS* 58 (1966), 679-680; Decree on the Missionary Activity of the Church *Ad Gentes* (7 December 1965), nn. 16 and 39: *AAS* 58 (1966), 966-967 and 986-987.

[27] Cf. C.I.C. can. 233, § 1; *Optatam Totius*, n. 2: *AAS* 58 (1966), 714-715; *Presbyterorum Ordinis*, n. 11: *AAS* 58 (1966), 1008-1009; *Lumen Gentium*, n. 11: *AAS* 57 (1965), 15-16; *Christus Dominus*, n. 15: *AAS* 58 (1966), 679-680; *Ad Gentes*, n. 39: *AAS* 58 (1966), 986-987; *Perfectae Caritatis*, n. 24: AAS 58 (1966), 711-712; Second Vatican Ecumenical Council, Pastoral Constitution on the Church in the Modern World *Gaudium et Spes* (7 December 1965), n. 52: AAS 58 (1966), 1073-1074; Decree on the Apostolate of the Laity *Apostolicam Actuositatem* (18 November 1965), n. 11: *AAS* 58 (1966), 847-849; Pius XII, Apostolic Exhortation to the Clergy of the Entire World on the Development of Holiness in Priestly Life *Menti Nostrae* (23 September 1950), Ch. III: *AAS* 42 (1950), 683.

atmosphere, which predispose a man to discernment and to accepting a priestly vocation.[28]

Thus understood, the pastoral care of vocations is aimed at men from a variety of age groups. Today, given the growth in mature vocations among those with one or more work experiences behind them[29], there is a growing awareness of the need to give particular attention to this age group.

15. With generosity and an ecclesial spirit, vocations should be promoted not just for one's own diocese or country, but also for the benefit of other particular Churches, according to the needs of the Universal Church. We should cooperate with the grace of God, which freely calls some to priestly ministry in a particular Church, others to exercise ministry in an Institute of Consecrated Life or in a Society of Apostolic Life, and others again to the *missio ad gentes*. It is greatly to be desired, therefore, that, in every diocese, there should be a single office for the pastoral care of vocations, which is an expression of the cooperation and unity between the diocesan Clergy and the clergy belonging to other canonically recognised ecclesial entities.[30]

(B) MINOR SEMINARIES AND OTHER FORMS OF ACCOMPANIMENT FOR ADOLESCENTS

16. The pastoral care of vocations seeks to recognise and accompany the response that is made to the interior call of the Lord. This process must foster the growth of the human and spiritual qualities of the person, and

---

[28] FRANCIS, Apostolic Exhortation *Evangelii Gaudium* (24 November 2013), n. 107: *AAS* 105 (2013), 1064-1065: "*Wherever there is life, fervour and a desire to bring Christ to others, genuine vocations will arise. Even in parishes where priests are not particularly committed or joyful, the fraternal life and fervour of the community can awaken in the young a desire to consecrate themselves completely to God and to the preaching of the Gospel. This is particularly true if such a living community prays insistently for vocations and courageously proposes to its young people the path of special consecration*".

[29] Cf. C.I.C., cann. 233, § 2; 385; cf. *Menti Nostrae*, Ch. III: *AAS* 42 (1950), 684; *Apostolorum Successores*, n. 87: *Enchiridion Vaticanum* 22 (2006), 1773; S. CONGREGATION FOR CATHOLIC EDUCATION, Circular Letter *Vocationes Adultorum*, to the Presidents of Conferences of Bishops on the Formation of Mature Vocations (14 July 1976): *Enchiridion Vaticanum* 5 (2000), 2097-2108.

[30] Cf. *Optatam Totius*, n. 2: *AAS* 58 (1966), 714-715; *Presbyterorum Ordinis*, nn. 10-11: *AAS* 58 (1966), 1007-1010; *Apostolorum Successores*, n. 91: *Enchiridion Vaticanum* 22 (2006), 1787-1789.

evaluate the authenticity of his motives. For these reasons, it is fitting that institutions suitable for the support and discernment of vocations to the ministerial priesthood should be encouraged in each particular Church. These must take into account its circumstances, means and acquired experience, along with the age and particular circumstances of those who will be formed there.

17. *The Minor Seminary*.[31] The *Code of Canon Law* states: "*Minor seminaries and other similar institutions are to be preserved, where they exist, and fostered; for the sake of fostering vocations, these institutions provide special religious formation together with instruction in the humanities and science. Where the diocesan bishop judges it expedient, he is to erect a minor seminary or similar institution*".[32]

18. The purpose of the minor seminary is to assist the human and Christian growth of adolescents[33], who manifest the seeds of a vocation to the ministerial priesthood. It develops, in a way appropriate to their age, that interior freedom by which they can make a response to the plan of God for their lives.

In places where this service is not provided institutionally in a minor seminary, each local Church should take on the important task of accompanying adolescents, by promoting new approaches and experimenting with creative pastoral initiatives, so as to help and direct their human and spiritual growth. Among many examples that can be named are *youth vocations groups*, *communities for vocational discernment*, *Catholic colleges*, and other youth organisations.[34]

19. In minor seminaries the qualities of the young men must be considered, along with the specific "signs of a vocation". Concretely, it will be of great help to evaluate previous experiences that have marked the life of

---

[31] Cf. *Optatam Totius*, n. 3: *AAS* 58 (1966), 715-716; *Pastores Dabo Vobis*, n. 63: *AAS* 84 (1992), 768-769.

[32] C.I.C., can. 234, § 1; cf. also *Apostolorum Successores*, n. 86: *Enchiridion Vaticanum* 22 (2006), 1770-1772.

[33] Cf. *Apostolorum Successores*, n. 86.

[34] Cf. *Pastores Dabo Vobis*, n. 64: *AAS* 84 (1992), 769-770.

faith of the young men. Examples of this would be the spiritual bond with a priest; frequent recourse to the sacraments; the beginnings of a prayer life; the ecclesial experience of the parish or of groups, movements and associations; participation in vocational activities promoted by the diocese; undertaking some task in the service of the ecclesial reality to which they belong. It is also necessary to consider some human qualities which, if they were suitably developed, can help the young men to advance in their vocational maturity. It is for the formators, therefore, to verify the overall suitability of those who might become candidates (spiritual, physical, psychological, moral and intellectual).

20. During the vocational journey of the minor seminary, it will be necessary to take into account the growth dynamic of the person, in a way that is age-appropriate and pays particular attention to the following aspects: sincerity and ease with himself and others, gradual emotional development, openness to live in community, capacity for cultivating brotherly friendships, a sense of responsibility about his own duties and the tasks entrusted to him, creativity and a spirit of initiative, the right expression of freedom, openness to a journey of prayer and of encounter with Christ.

21. By experiencing friendship with Jesus, the young men should learn to live and develop their fidelity to the Lord, supported by prayer and by the strength of the Holy Spirit. In this way they are to mature in humble service, understood as availability to others and concern for the common good; obedience, lived as a trustful listening; youthful chastity, as a sign of the transparency of relationships and the gift of self; and poverty, as a formation in the temperate use of material things and in a life of simplicity.

An essential element of this spiritual formation is the liturgical and sacramental life, in which the young will have to participate ever more consciously, in accordance with their age, as they grow up. Another important element is Marian devotion and other pious exercises practised daily or periodically, to be set out, like all the other matters, in the Rule of Life of each seminary.

22. Young people should receive the education required by their own country for entrance to university.[35] Moreover, they should seek to obtain state-recognised academic qualifications, which will also allow them the freedom and the possibility of choosing another state of life, if it were to transpire that they were not called to the priesthood. It would also be fitting for the seminary to offer a complementary formation, which would take into account, for example, culture, art and sport, etc. Studies can take place either in the school of the seminary itself, in some other Catholic school or elsewhere.

23. Given the importance and the need for a challenging formation during adolescence, in which the identities of the young men begin to mature, it is necessary that they be accompanied by formators who understand the requirements of their age and who are good educators and witnesses of the Gospel. It is desirable that formators can work together with parents who, at this stage above all, have a fundamental role in the process of growth of their sons. It is likewise desirable to have the support and involvement of their home parish communities. Moreover, formators should take care that seminarians maintain suitable, and also necessary, relationships with their own families and with their peers. They will need such relationships for a healthy psychological development, especially where the affective life is concerned.

(C) MATURE VOCATIONS

24. Those who discover the call to ministerial priesthood at a more advanced age come with a more developed personality and a life journey characterised by a range of experiences. Their initial admission to seminary should be preceded by a spiritual and ecclesial programme, in which a serious discernment of the motivations in responding to a vocation can be undertaken.

It is necessary to assess carefully the interval between Baptism or Christian conversion and entry into the seminary[36], since it is not unusual to encounter confusion between the *sequela Christi* and the call to ministerial priesthood.

---

[35] Cf. C.I.C., can. 234, § 2.
[36] Cf. *ibid.*, can. 1042, n. 3.

As in the case of other seminarians, these candidates should be accompanied in a serious and comprehensive journey, which should include, in the context of a community life, a solid spiritual and theological formation[37], using appropriate pedagogical and didactic methods, that take account of the personal profile of each man. It will be the competence of the Conferences of Bishops to issue specific norms appropriate for their own national situation, assessing whether to establish an age limit for the admission of such vocations, and considering whether to establish a separate seminary for them.[38]

(D) VOCATIONS ARISING AMONG INDIGENOUS PEOPLES

25. "Special attention needs to be given to vocations among indigenous peoples: they need a formation which takes account of their culture. While receiving a proper theological and pastoral formation for their future ministry, these candidates for the priesthood should not be uprooted from their own culture".[39] The very presence of such vocations is an important element of the inculturation of the Gospel in these regions, and the richness of their culture must be adequately respected. Vocational assistance can be provided in the native language whenever necessary, placing this in the context of the local culture.

(E) VOCATIONS AND MIGRANTS

26. The phenomenon of migration is becoming quite widespread for a variety of reasons of a social, economic, political and religious nature.[40] It is important that Christian communities offer constant pastoral care of immigrant families that live and work in their country for a time. These families are a valuable resource for them. Vocations to the priestly ministry can arise from within these families,

---

[37] Cf. *Pastores Dabo Vobis*, n. 64: *AAS* 84 (1992), 769-770; *Vocationes Adultorum*, n. 12: *Enchiridion Vaticanum* 5 (2000), 2102.

[38] Cf. *Apostolorum Successores*, n. 87.

[39] JOHN PAUL II, Post-Synodal Apostolic Exhortation *Ecclesia in America* (22 January 1999), n. 40: *AAS* 91 (1999), 776.

[40] Cf. FRANCIS, Post-Synodal Apostolic Exhortation *Amoris Laetitia* (19 March 2016), n. 46, Libreria Editrice Vaticana 2016.

which must be accompanied, keeping in mind the need for a gradual cultural integration.[41]

27. There are others who, feeling called by the Lord, leave their own country, in order to receive formation for the priesthood elsewhere. It is important to pay attention to their personal history and to the background from which they have come, and to assess carefully the motivations for their vocational choice, establishing a dialogue with their Church of origin whenever possible. In any case, during the process of formation it will be necessary to find ways and means to ensure an adequate integration, without underestimating the challenge of cultural differences, which can, at times, make vocational discernment rather complex.

---

[41] Cf. PONTIFICAL COUNCIL FOR THE PASTORAL CARE OF MIGRANTS AND ITINERANT PEOPLES, Instruction *Erga Migrantes Caritas Christi* (3 May 2004), n. 45: *Enchiridion Vaticanum* 22 (2006), 2480-2481.

III. THE FOUNDATIONS OF FORMATION

(A) THE SUBJECT OF FORMATION

28. During the process of formation for the ministerial priesthood, the seminarian is a "mystery to himself", in which two aspects of his humanity, that need to be integrated, are intertwined and exist side by side. On the one hand he is characterised by talents and gifts that have been moulded by grace; on the other he is marked by his limits and frailty. The task of formation is to help the person to integrate these aspects, under the influence of the Holy Spirit, in a journey of faith and of gradual and harmonious maturity, avoiding fragmentation, polarisation, excesses, superficiality or partiality. The time of formation for priestly ministry is a period of testing, maturing and discernment by both the seminarian and the house of formation.

29. The seminarian is called to "go out of himself"[42], to make his way, in Christ, towards the Father and towards others, embracing the call to priesthood, dedicating himself to work with the Holy Spirit, to achieve a serene and creative interior synthesis between strength and weakness. The educational endeavour helps seminarians to bring all aspects of their personality to Christ, in this way making them consciously free for God and for others.[43] In fact it is only in the crucified and risen Christ that this path of integration finds meaning and completion; all things are united in him (cf. *Eph* 1:10), so that *"God might be all in all"* (cf. *1 Cor* 15:28).

---

[42] Cf. FRANCIS, *Address to Seminarians and Novices from Various Countries of the World on the Occasion of the Year of Faith* (6 July 2013): *Insegnamenti* I/2 (2013), 13.

[43] Cf. S. CONGREGATION FOR CATHOLIC EDUCATION, *Guidelines for Formation in Priestly Celibacy* (11 April 1974), n. 38: *Enchiridion Vaticanum* 5 (2000), 275-276 [English Translation: *Origins* 4:5 (27 June 1974), 66-76]; and CONGREGATION FOR CATHOLIC EDUCATION, *Guidelines for the Use of Psychology in the Admission and Formation of Candidates for the Priesthood* (29 June 2008), n. 9: *Enchiridion Vaticanum* 25 (2011), 1268-1269.

(B) THE BASIS AND THE PURPOSE OF FORMATION: PRIESTLY IDENTITY

30. For an integrated formation of the candidate, it is necessary to reflect on the identity of the priest.[44] A first consideration must be theological in nature, since the vocation to priesthood is rooted, and finds its *raison d'être*, in God and in his loving plan. Jesus brings about the new covenant by his self-offering and his blood, in this way giving birth to a messianic people that is "a *lasting and sure seed of unity, hope and salvation for the whole human race*".[45] As the Second Vatican Council reminds us, the nature and mission of priests must be understood within the Church, the People of God, the Body of Christ, the Temple of the Holy Spirit[46], for the service of which they consecrate their lives.

31. The entire community of believers is constituted, through the anointing of the Holy Spirit, as a visible sacrament for the salvation of the world. The entire People of God, in fact, participates in the saving work of Christ[47], a priestly people offering a *"living sacrifice acceptable to God"* (cf. *Rom* 12:1).[48] The unity and dignity of the baptismal vocation precede any differentiation in ministry. The Second Vatican Council, in fact, states that, *"Though they differ from one another in essence and not only in degree, the common priesthood of the faithful and the ministerial or hierarchical priesthood are nonetheless interrelated: each of them in its own special way is a participation in the one priesthood of Christ"*.[49] The ministerial priesthood, therefore, is understood, both in its own specific nature and in its biblical and theological foundations, as a service to the glory of God and to the brothers and sisters in their baptismal priesthood.[50]

---

[44] Cf. CONGREGATION FOR THE CLERGY, *Directory for the Ministry and Life of Priests* (11 February 2013), Ch. I.

[45] *Lumen Gentium*, n. 9: *AAS* 57 (1965), 13.

[46] Cf. *ibid.*, n. 17: *AAS* 57 (1965), 21.

[47] Cf. *ibid.*, n. 10: *AAS* 57 (1965), 14-15; C.I.C., can. 204, § 1.

[48] Cf. *1 Pt* 2:4-9.

[49] *Lumen Gentium*, n. 10: *AAS* 57 (1965), 14.

[50] Cf. *ibid.*, nn. 10 e 18: *AAS* 57 (1965), 14-15 and 21-22; *Presbyterorum Ordinis*, n. 2: *AAS* 58 (1966), 991-993; *Catechism of the Catholic Church*, nn. 1547 and 1592.

32. Every believer is anointed by the Holy Spirit, and actively participates in the mission of the Church according to his own proper charisms. At the same time, it is also true that *"the same Lord, however, has established ministers among his faithful to unite them together in one body in which, 'not all the members have the same function'* (*Rom* 12:4). *These ministers in the society of the faithful are able by the sacred power of orders to offer sacrifice and to forgive sins, and they perform their priestly office publicly for men in the name of Christ"*[51]. This means that, in communion with the order of bishops, priests are inseparably part of the ecclesial community and, at the same time, by the will of Christ and in continuance of the work of the Apostles, have been constituted to be pastors and leaders. Thus, *"the priest is placed not only in the Church but also in the forefront of the Church"*.[52]

33. As a member of the holy People of God, the priest is called to cultivate his missionary zeal, exercising his pastoral responsibility with humility as an authoritative leader, teacher of the Word and minister of the sacraments[53], practising his spiritual fatherhood fruitfully.

Consequently, future priests should be educated so that they do not become prey to "clericalism", nor yield to the temptation of modelling their lives on the search for popular consensus. This would inevitably lead them to fall short in exercising their ministry as leaders of the community, leading them to think about the Church as a merely human institution.

34. On the other hand, priestly ordination, which has made him a leader of the people, by the outpouring of the Holy Spirit through the imposition of hands by the bishop, should not lead him to "lord it over" the flock (cf. *1 Pt* 5:3): *"Indeed, every authority is exercised in a spirit of service as 'amoris officium' and unpretentious dedication for the good of the flock"*[54].

---

[51] *Presbyterorum Ordinis*, n. 2: *AAS* 58 (1966), 992.

[52] *Pastores Dabo Vobis*, n. 16: *AAS* 84 (1992), 681.

[53] Cf. CONGREGATION FOR THE CLERGY, *The Priest and the Third Christian Millennium. Teacher of the Word, Minister of the Sacraments and Leader of the Community* (19 March 1999), *Enchiridion Vaticanum* 18 (2002), 289-376.

[54] *Directory for the Ministry and Life of Priests*, n. 25; cf. also Mt 20:25-28 and Mk 10:42-45; Francis, *General Audience* (26 March 2014): *L'Osservatore Romano* 70 (27 March 2014), 8.

In conclusion, the priestly vocation begins with the gift of divine grace, which is then sealed in sacramental ordination. This gift is expressed over time through the mediation of the Church, which calls and sends in the name of God. At the same time, the personal response develops through a process, which begins with an awareness of the gift received, and matures gradually with the help of priestly spirituality, until it becomes a stable way of life, with its own obligations and rights, and a specific mission accepted by the one ordained.

(C) THE JOURNEY OF FORMATION AS CONFIGURATION TO CHRIST

35. Priests, who are configured to Christ, Head and Shepherd, Servant and Spouse[55], participate in his one priesthood and saving mission as co-workers with the bishops. In this way they are visible signs of the merciful love of the Father in the Church and in the world. These characteristics of the person of Christ help us to understand better the ministerial priesthood in the Church. Under the guidance of the Holy Spirit, they inspire and guide the formation of seminarians, so that they can be conformed to Christ by their immersion in the mystery of the Trinity.[56]

36. The Letter to the Hebrews presents Christ's priesthood as an expression of his mission to all people.[57] The first quality that characterises Christ as true High Priest is his singular closeness both to God and to humanity.[58] Christ, who is full of mercy, is the priest who is *"holy, innocent and undefiled"* (cf. Heb 7:26) who, having offered himself *"with loud cries and tears"* (5:7), *"is able to deal patiently"* (5:2) with our every weakness, and becomes *"the source of eternal salvation for all those who obey him"* (5:9).

True God and true man, Christ brought to fulfilment, in love, the realities that preceded him: priesthood (cf. Heb 7:1-28), covenant (cf. 8:1-9,28), sacrifice (cf. 10:1-18). The sacrifice offered by Christ the

---

[55] Cf. *Presbyterorum Ordinis*, n. 2: *AAS* 58 (1966), 991-993; *Pastores Dabo Vobis*, n. 3: *AAS* 84 (1992), 660-662; *Directory for the Ministry and Life of Priests*, n. 6.

[56] Cf. *Presbyterorum Ordinis*, n. 2: *AAS* 58 (1966), 991-993.

[57] Cf. Benedict XVI, *Meeting with Parish Priests of the Diocese of Rome* (18 February 2010): *Insegnamenti* VI/1 (2010), 243.

[58] Cf. *Pastores Dabo Vobis*, n. 13: *AAS* 84 (1992), 677-678.

Priest was new in a particular way: he did not offer the blood of goats or of calves, but his own blood, to do the will of the Father. The words of Jesus in the Upper Room, *"This is my body, which will be given for you; do this in memory of me [...] This cup is the new covenant in my blood, which will be shed for you"* (cf. *Lk* 22:19-20), explain *"the particular interplay between the Eucharist and the priesthood [...]: these two Sacraments were born together and their destiny is indissolubly linked until the end of the world"*.[59] The ministry and life of the priest are, therefore, essentially rooted in the Eucharist.

37. He who gives his own life as a sacrifice presents himself as the Good Shepherd[60], who has come to gather together the scattered sheep of the house of Israel, and to lead them into the sheepfold of the Kingdom of God (cf. *Mt* 9:36; *Mk* 6:34). With this image, used widely in salvation history, Christ reveals that God is the one who gathers, accompanies, follows and cares for his own flock. Here we see the image of a Shepherd-God, who shares our life to the point of taking upon himself our suffering and our death.[61]

38. Jesus, the Son of God, has assumed the condition of a slave even unto death (cf. *Phil* 2:6-8). Before dying on the cross, he washed the feet of his disciples, commanding them to do the same (cf. *Jn* 13:1-17). The bond between priestly ministry and the mission of Christ seems particularly evocative in light of the so-called fourth song of the suffering servant of the Prophet Isaiah (cf. *Is* 52:13-53,12). The suffering servant prefigures what he himself will accomplish for humanity by his compassionate sharing of suffering and death, even to the giving of his own life on the cross (cf. *Is* 53:4-8).

39. Priestly ordination requires, in the one who receives it, a complete giving of himself for the service of the People of God, as an image of

---

[59] JOHN PAUL II, *Letter to Priests for Holy Thursday* (28 March 2004): *Insegnamenti* XXVII/1 (2004), 390.
[60] Cf. *Pastores Dabo Vobis*, n. 22: *AAS* 84 (1992), 690-691.
[61] Cf. BENEDICT XVI, Encyclical Letter *Spe Salvi* (30 November 2007), n. 6: *AAS* 99 (2007), 990-991.

Christ the Spouse: *"Christ's gift of himself to his Church, the fruit of his love, is described in terms of that unique gift of self made by the bridegroom to the bride"*.[62] The priest is called to have within himself the same feelings and attitudes that Christ has towards the Church, loved tenderly through the exercise of the ministry. Thus, he is required to *"be capable of loving people with a heart which is new, generous and pure - with genuine self-detachment, with full, constant and faithful dedication and at the same time with a kind of 'divine jealousy'* (cf. 2 Cor 11:2) *and even with a kind of maternal tenderness"*.[63]

40. The priest is, therefore, called to form himself so that his heart and his life are conformed to the Lord Jesus, in this way becoming a sign of the love God has for each person. By being intimately united to Christ, he will be able: to preach the Gospel and become an instrument of the mercy of God; to guide and give correction; to intercede and care for the spiritual life of the faithful entrusted to him; to listen and welcome, while also responding to the demands and the deep questions of our time.[64]

(D) A FORMATION FOR INTERIOR LIFE AND COMMUNION

41. The pastoral care of the faithful demands that the priest have a solid formation and interior maturity. He cannot limit himself simply to demonstrating a "veneer of virtuous habits", a merely external and formalistic obedience to abstract principles. Rather, he is called to act with great interior freedom. Indeed, it is expected of him that, day after day, he will internalise the spirit of the Gospel, thanks to a constant and personal friendship with Christ, leading him to share his sentiments and his attitudes.

---

[62] *Pastores Dabo Vobis*, n. 22: AAS 84 (1992), 691.

[63] *Ibid.*

[64] FRANCIS, *Address to the Rectors and Students of the Pontifical Colleges and Residences of Rome* (12 May 2014): *L'Osservatore Romano* 108 (14 May 2014), 5: "Sometimes, the pastor must go in front in order to indicate the way; at other times, must be among them to find out what is happening; and many times behind, to help those who are falling behind and also to follow the scent of the sheep that know where the good grass is"; cf. also Id., *General Audience*, 26 March 2014: *L'Osservatore Romano* 70 (27 March 2014), 8; *Address to the Priests of the Diocese of Rome* (6 March 2014): *L'Osservatore Romano* 54 (7 March 2014), 8.

Thus, by growing in charity, the future priest must seek to develop a balanced and mature capacity to enter into relationship with his neighbour. Indeed, he is called above all to a basic human and spiritual serenity[65] that, by overcoming every form of self-promotion or emotional dependency, allows him to be a man of communion, of mission and of dialogue.[66] In contemplating the Lord, who offered his life for others, he will be able to give himself generously and with self-sacrifice for the People of God.

42. To be formed in the spirit of the Gospel, the interior man needs to take special and faithful care of the interior spiritual life, centred principally on communion with Christ through the mysteries celebrated in the course of the liturgical year, and nourished by personal prayer and meditation on the inspired Word. In silent prayer, which opens him to an authentic relationship with Christ, the seminarian becomes docile to the action of the Spirit, which gradually moulds him in the image of the Master. By this intimate relationship with the Lord and by their fraternal communion, seminarians will be helped to recognise and correct "spiritual worldliness": obsession with personal appearances, a presumed theological or disciplinary certainty, narcissism and authoritarianism, the attempt to dominate others, a merely external and ostentatious preoccupation with the liturgy, vainglory, individualism, the inability to listen to others, and every form of careerism.[67] They should instead be formed in simplicity, sobriety, serene dialogue and authenticity. As disciples at the school of the Master, they should learn to live and act with the pastoral charity that flows from being "*servants of Christ and stewards of the mysteries of God*" (cf. *1 Cor* 4:1).

43. Priestly formation is a journey of transformation that renews the heart and mind of the person, so that he can "*discern what is the will of God, what is good and pleasing and perfect*" (cf. *Rom* 12:2). Indeed, the gradual inner growth along the journey of formation should principally be aimed at making the future priest a "man of discernment", able to read the

---

[65] Cf. Id., *Address to the Participants in the Convention Sponsored by the Congregation for the Clergy on the 50th Anniversary of the Conciliar Decrees "Optatam Totius" and "Presbyterorum Ordinis"* (20 November 2015): *L'Osservatore Romano* 267 (21 November 2015), 8.
[66] Cf. *Pastores Dabo Vobis*, n. 18: *AAS* 84 (1992), 684-686.
[67] Cf. *Evangelii Gaudium*, nn. 93-97: *AAS* 105 (2013), 1059-1061.

reality of human life in the light of the Spirit. In this way he will be able to choose, decide and act according to the will of God.

The first area of discernment is the personal life. It is necessary to integrate one's own personal situation and history into the spiritual life. This will ensure that the vocation to the priesthood does not become imprisoned in an abstract ideal, nor run the risk of reducing itself to a merely practical and organisational activism, removed from the conscience of the person. Discerning one's life according to the Gospel means cultivating every day a deep spiritual life, so as to receive it and interpret it with full responsibility, and a growing trust in God, directing the heart towards him each day.[68]

This means working humbly and ceaselessly on oneself - something that goes beyond mere introspection - so that the priest opens himself honestly to the truths of life and to the real demands of ministry. He learns to listen to the conscience that judges his movements and the interior urges that motivate his actions. In this way, the priest learns to govern himself using the spiritual and mental powers of mind and body. He grasps the sense of what can be done and what it would be better not to do, or what should not be done. He begins to organise his energies, his plans and his duties with a balanced self-discipline and an honest awareness of his own limits and abilities. This work cannot be undertaken satisfactorily by relying only on his own human resources. On the contrary, it relies principally on welcoming the gift of divine grace, that enables him to transcend himself, to go beyond his own needs and external conditioning, to live in the freedom of the children of God. It is a way of "looking within" and a holistic spiritual outlook, which directs the whole of his life and ministry. In this way he learns how to act with prudence, and to judge the consequences of his actions beyond certain limited circumstances that can impede a clear judgement of things.

This journey of being honest with oneself calls for a special care of the inner life by personal prayer, spiritual direction, daily contact with the Word of God, the contemplation of the priestly life in a spirit of faith along with other priests and the bishop, and all the other means that help to cultivate the virtues of prudence and right judgement. In this ongoing

---

[68] This is *"the fundamental question of our priestly life: Where is my heart directed? It is a question we need to keep asking, daily, weekly... Where is my heart directed?"*, FRANCIS, *Homily for the Jubilee of Priests and Seminarians* (3 June 2016). *L'Osservatore Romano* 126 (4 June 2016), 8.

path of discernment, the priest will learn how to interpret and understand his own motivations, his gifts, his needs and his frailties, so as to *"free himself from all disordered affections and, having removed them, to seek out and find the will of God in the ordering of his life with a view to the salvation of the soul"*.[69]

(E) MEANS OF FORMATION

e.1. Personal Accompaniment[70]

44. Seminarians need to be accompanied in a personal way in the various stages of their journey by those entrusted with the work of formation, each according to his proper role and competence. The purpose of personal accompaniment is to carry out vocational discernment and to form the missionary disciple.

45. In the process of formation, it is necessary that the seminarian should know himself and let himself be known, relating to the formators with sincerity and transparency.[71] Personal accompaniment, which has *docibilitas* to the Holy Spirit as its goal, is an indispensable means of formation.

46. Conversations with formators should be regular and frequent. In this way the seminarian will be able gradually to conform himself to Christ, docile to the action of the Spirit. Such accompaniment must bring together all the aspects of the human person, training him in listening, in dialogue, in the true meaning of obedience and in interior freedom. It is the task of every formator, each according to his proper responsibilities, to assist the seminarian in becoming aware of his condition, of the talents that he has received, and of his frailties, so that he can become ever more receptive to the action of grace.

47. A necessary element in the process of accompaniment is mutual trust.[72] The programme of formation should explore and outline the

---

[69] Ignatius of Loyola, *Spiritual Exercises*, 1.

[70] Cf. Francis, *Evangelii Gaudium*, nn. 169-173: *AAS* 105 (2013), 1091-1092.

[71] Cf. Francis, *Address to Seminarians and Novices from Various Countries of the World on the Occasion of the Year of Faith* (6 July 2013): *Insegnamenti* I/2 (2013), 9.

[72] Cf. *Guidelines for the Use of Psychology in the Admission and Formation of Candidates for the Priesthood*, n. 12: *Enchiridion Vaticanum* 25 (2011), 1273-1277.

concrete ways in which this trust can be encouraged and safeguarded. Above all, those conditions should be sought and fostered, which can, in some way, create a peaceful climate of trust and mutual confidence: fraternity, empathy, understanding, the ability to listen and to share, and especially a coherent witness of life.

48. Accompaniment must be present from the beginning of the journey of formation and throughout life, even if it requires different approaches after ordination. A serious discernment of the vocational situation of the candidate at the outset will avoid needless procrastination when it comes to making a judgement about suitability for priestly ministry. This will avoid leading the candidate to the threshold of ordination, without having ascertained whether the indispensable conditions have been met.[73]

49. The formator must exercise discretion when it comes to the lives of seminarians. Each formator should be possessed of human[74], spiritual[75], pastoral and professional abilities and resources, so as to provide the right kind of accompaniment that is balanced and respectful of the freedom and the conscience of the other person, and that will help him in his human and spiritual growth. Moreover, those who are marked out to become formators need a specific preparation[76] and generous dedication to this important task. Formators are needed who can ensure their full-time presence and who, above all else, are witnesses of how to love and serve the people of God, giving themselves without reserve for the Church.[77]

---

[73] Cf. *ibid.*, nn. 8 and 11: *Enchiridion Vaticanum* 25 (2011), 1262-1267.

[74] Cf. *ibid.*, nn. 3-4.

[75] Cf. CONGREGATION FOR CATHOLIC EDUCATION, Circular Letter *Concerning Some More Urgent Aspects of Spiritual Formation in Seminaries* (6 January 1980): *Enchiridion Vaticanum* 7 (2001), 45-90. [English Translation: *Origins* 9:38 (6 March 1980) 610-619].

[76] Cf. Id., *Directives Concerning the Preparation of Seminary Educators* (4 November 1993): *Enchiridion Vaticanum* 13 (1996), 3151-3284. [English Translation: *Origins* 23:22 (27 January 1994) 557-571]; cf. also *Pastores Dabo Vobis*, n. 66: *AAS* 84 (1992), 772-774.

[77] Cf. *Directives Concerning the Preparation of Seminary Educators*, nn. 4.19.29-32.66: *Enchiridion Vaticanum* 13 (1996), 3155; 3184; 3200-3207; 3260-3262. [English Translation: *Origins* 23:22 (27 January 1994) 557-571]; *Apostolorum Successores*, n. 89: *Enchiridion Vaticanum* 22 (2006), 1777-1780.

e.2. Community Accompaniment

50. A healthy pedagogy of formation will not neglect to pay attention to the experience and dynamic of the group of which the seminarian forms a part. Community life during the years of initial formation must make an impact on each individual, purifying his intentions and transforming the conduct of his life as he gradually conforms himself to Christ. Formation comes about every day through interpersonal relationships, moments of exchange and discussion which result in the development of that "fertile soil", in which a vocation matures concretely.

51. A community environment of this kind will benefit future relationships with the bishop, with the brothers in the priesthood and with the lay faithful. The experience of community life is a valuable element that cannot be neglected in the formation of those who will be called, in the future, to exercise a true spiritual fatherhood[78] in the communities entrusted to them. Each candidate who prepares for ministry is bound to aspire ever more deeply to communion.[79]

The spirit of communion is rooted in the fact that the Church, as a people brought together by Christ, is called to live a strong experience of community life, as it has done from the beginning.[80] Indeed, one must remember that, after their priestly ordination, priests are *"united among themselves in an intimate sacramental brotherhood"* and *"in individual dioceses, priests form one priesthood under their own bishop"*.[81] By virtue of his ordination, the priest becomes part of a family, of which the bishop is the father.[82]

52. In the Church, which is *"the home and the school of communion"*[83] and which *"derives its unity from the unity of the Father, the Son and the*

---

[78] Cf. Francis, *Address to Seminarians and Novices from Various Countries of the World on the Occasion of the Year of Faith* (6 July 2013): *Insegnamenti* I/2 (2013), 8.

[79] Cf. *Pastores Dabo Vobis*, nn. 17; 22-23; 43.59: *AAS* 84 (1992), 682-684; 690-694; 731-733; 761-762.

[80] Cf. *Acts* 2:42.

[81] *Presbyterorum Ordinis*, n. 8: *AAS* 58 (1966), 1003.

[82] Cf. *Christus Dominus*, nn. 16 and 28: *AAS* 58 (1966), 680-681 and 687; *Apostolorum Successores*, nn. 76 and 107: *Enchiridion Vaticanum* 22 (2006), 1740-1742 and 1827-1828.

[83] John Paul II, Apostolic Letter *Novo Millennio Ineunte* (6 January 2001), n. 43: *AAS* 93 (2001), 297.

Holy Spirit"[84], the priest is called to be a *"man of communion"*[85]. Consequently, the bonds that are created in the seminary between formators and seminarians, and between the seminarians themselves, must be marked by a sense of fatherhood and fraternity.[86] In fact, fraternity is fostered through spiritual growth, which requires a constant effort to overcome various forms of individualism. A fraternal relationship *"cannot just be left to chance, to fortuitous circumstances"*[87], but is rather a conscious choice and an ongoing challenge.

The seminary community is indeed a family, marked by an atmosphere that favours friendship and fraternity. Such an experience will help the seminarian in the future to understand better the demands, the dynamics and also the problems of the families entrusted to his pastoral care.[88] In this respect, it will be good for the seminary community to open itself up to welcoming and engaging with various groups, for instance families, consecrated persons, young people, students, and the poor.

(F) THE UNITY OF FORMATION

53. Since it should be an ongoing experience of discipleship, formation is a single and integrated path, beginning in seminary and continuing into priestly life, where it takes the form of ongoing formation. At each stage it requires care and attention. Even if *"much of the effectiveness of the training offered depends on the maturity and strength of personality of those entrusted with formation"*[89], one must always keep in mind that the seminarian first - and later the priest - *"is a necessary and irreplaceable agent in his own formation"*.[90]

---

[84] CYPRIAN, *De Dominica Oratione* 23: CSEL III A, p. 285.

[85] *Pastores Dabo Vobis*, n. 18: *AAS* 84 (1992), 684.

[86] Cf. *ibid.*, n. 60: *AAS* 84 (1992), 764-772; FRANCIS, *Address to Seminarians and Novices from Various Countries of the World on the Occasion of the Year of Faith* (6 July 2013): *Insegnamenti* I/2 (2013), 11.

[87] FRANCIS, *Meeting with Diocesan Priests in the Cathedral of Cassano all'Jonio* (21 June 2014): *L'Osservatore Romano* 140 (22 June 2014), 7.

[88] Cf. CONGREGATION FOR CATHOLIC EDUCATION, *Directives on the Formation of Seminarians Concerning Problems Related to Marriage and the Family* (19 March 1995), n. 33. [English translation: *Origins* 25:10 (August 10, 1995) 161-167].

[89] *Pastores Dabo Vobis*, n. 66: *AAS* 84 (1992), 772-774.

[90] *Ibid.*, n. 69: *AAS* 84 (1992), 778.

IV. INITIAL AND ONGOING FORMATION

54. After the first, indispensable vocational discernment, formation - understood as one unbroken missionary journey of discipleship[91] - can be divided into two principal moments: initial formation in the seminary and ongoing formation in priestly life.

55. *Initial* formation concerns the time leading up to priestly ordination, from the beginning of the propaedeutic period, which is an integral part of it. Therefore, this time must be characterised by the elements of formation that prepare the seminarian for priestly life. This calls for patient and demanding work on the person, who is open to the action of the Holy Spirit. Its purpose is to form a priestly heart.

56. *Ongoing* formation is an indispensable requirement in the life of every priest and in his exercise of the priestly ministry. In fact, the interior attitude of the priest must be distinguished by an ongoing openness to the will of God, following the example of Christ. This implies a continuous conversion of heart, the capacity to see one's life and its events in the light of faith and, above all, of pastoral charity, by way of a total gift of self to the Church, according to the design of God.

This being understood, it is overly simplistic and erroneous to view ongoing formation as a simple "updating" in cultural and spiritual matters, relative to the initial formation of the seminary. Indeed, *"long-term preparation for ongoing formation should take place in the major seminary, where encouragement needs to be given to future priests to look forward to it, seeing its necessity, its advantages and the spirit in which*

---

[91] FRANCIS, *Letter to Participants in the Extraordinary General Assembly of the Italian Episcopal Conference* (8 November 2014): *L'Osservatore Romano* 258 (12 November 2014), 7: "*The formation of which we speak is an experience of permanent discipleship, which draws one close to Christ and allows one to be ever more conformed to him. Therefore, it has no end, for priests never stop being disciples of Jesus, they never stop following him. Thus, formation understood as discipleship sustains the ordained minister his entire life and regards his entire person and his ministry. Initial and ongoing formation are two aspects of one reality: the path of the disciple priest, in love with his Lord and steadfastly following him*".

it should be undertaken, and appropriate conditions for its realisation need to be ensured".[92]

(A) INITIAL FORMATION AND ITS STAGES

57. Initial formation can be further subdivided into four principal stages, whose characteristics will be outlined in greater detail below: the "propaedeutic stage", the "stage of philosophical studies" or "discipleship stage", the "stage of theological studies" or "configuration stage", and the "pastoral stage" or "stage of vocational synthesis". One is always a "disciple" throughout the whole of life, constantly aspiring to configure oneself to Christ, by exercising pastoral ministry. Indeed, these dimensions are a constant feature of the journey of each seminarian, but some receive greater attention at particular stages over the course of formation, albeit never to the neglect of the others.

58. At the conclusion of each stage, it is important to assess whether the aims of that particular period of formation have been achieved, taking account of periodic evaluations (preferably each semester, or at least annually), which the formators will prepare in writing. The attainment of formation objectives should not necessarily be tied to the time spent in the seminary and especially not to the studies completed. That is to say, one should not arrive "automatically" at the priesthood merely by reason of having followed a series of pre-established stages in chronological order and set out beforehand, independently of the actual progress that has been achieved in overall integral maturity. Rather, ordination is the goal of a genuinely completed spiritual journey, that has gradually helped the seminarian to become aware of the call he has received and the characteristics that pertain to priestly identity, allowing him to reach the necessary human, Christian and priestly maturity.

The community of formators must be coherent and objective in the periodic integral assessments they make of seminarians, taking account of the four dimensions of formation, which will be addressed in Chapter V. The seminarian is required to be docile, to review his own life constantly and to be open to fraternal correction, so as to respond ever more fully to the workings of grace.

---

[92] *Pastores Dabo Vobis*, n. 71: *AAS* 84 (1992), 783.

a.1. The Propaedeutic Stage

59. The experience of recent decades[93] has revealed the need to dedicate a period of time to preparation of an introductory nature, in view of the priestly formation to follow or, alternatively, of the decision to follow a different path in life. Ordinarily this period is not to be less than one year or more than two.

The propaedeutic stage is an indispensable phase of formation with its own specific character. Its principal objective is to provide a solid basis for the spiritual life and to nurture a greater self-awareness for personal growth. In order to launch and develop their spiritual life, it will be necessary to lead seminarians to prayer by way of the sacramental life; the Liturgy of the Hours; familiarity with the Word of God, which is to be considered the soul and guide of the journey; silence; mental prayer; and spiritual reading. Moreover, this time is an ideal opportunity to acquire an initial and overall familiarity with Christian doctrine by studying the *Catechism of the Catholic Church* and by developing the dynamic of self-giving through experiences in the parish setting and charitable works. Finally, if necessary, the propaedeutic stage can help to make up for anything that is missing in their general education.

The studies of the propaedeutic stage are always to be considered entirely distinct from philosophical studies.

60. The propaedeutic stage can be adapted according to the culture and experiences of the local Church. However, it must always be a real time of vocational discernment, undertaken within community life, and a "start" to the following stages of *initial formation*.

---

[93] The propaedeutic stage follows the preliminary discernment of a vocation and the first vocational accompaniment outside the seminary. Cf. *Pastores Dabo Vobis*, n. 62: *AAS* 84 (1992), 767-768. The Congregation for Catholic Education recommended, already by 1980, that this initial stage should be offered: "*The need to intensify the preparation of aspirants to major seminary has become pressing, not only from an intellectual point of view but also, and more especially, from the human and spiritual perspectives*", CONGREGATION FOR CATHOLIC EDUCATION, Information Document *The Propaedeutic Period* (10 May 1998), III, n. 1. The Congregation for the Evangelisation of Peoples, in a circular letter of 25 April 1987, expressed its hope that the propaedeutic period might be "*a prolonged period of vocational discernment, of growth in the spiritual life and community life and, if needs be, a period in which cultural preparation can be supplemented with a view to the study of philosophy and theology*": *Enchiridion Vaticanum* 10 (1989), 1214.

In the formation that is offered, emphasis should be placed on communion with one's bishop, with the presbyterate and with the entire particular Church, especially as quite a few vocations nowadays originate within various groups and movements, and so need to develop deeper bonds with the diocese.[94]

It is fitting that the propaedeutic stage be lived in a community distinct from the major seminary and, where at all possible, that it should have its own house. A propaedeutic programme should be developed, therefore, with its own formators to provide a solid human and Christian formation and a careful selection of candidates for major seminary.[95]

a.2. The Stage of Philosophical Studies (or Discipleship)

61. *The concept of discipleship.* The disciple is the one whom the Lord has called to "stay with him" (cf. *Mk* 3:14), to follow him, and to become a missionary of the Gospel. Each day he learns how to enter into the secrets of the Kingdom of God, living a deep relationship with Jesus. Staying with Christ becomes a pedagogical-spiritual journey, that transforms the life of the seminarian and bears witness to his love in the world.

62. The experience and dynamic of discipleship, that lasts, as we have noted, for the whole of life, and includes all priestly formation, pedagogically requires a specific stage in which all possible efforts are expended to root the seminarian in the *sequela Christi*, listening to his Word, keeping it in his heart and putting it into practice. This specific period is characterised by the formation of the disciple of Jesus who is destined to be a pastor. Special attention is given to the human dimension, in harmony with spiritual growth, so as to help the seminarian mature in his definitive decision to follow the Lord in ministerial priesthood, by embracing the evangelical counsels in a way proper to this stage.

---

[94] Cf. The *Propaedeutic Period*, III, n. 5.

[95] Francis, *Address to the Plenary of the Congregation for the Clergy* (3 October 2014): *L'Osservatore Romano* 226 (4 October 2014), 8: "*one must carefully study the evolution of a vocation! See whether it comes from the Lord, whether the man is healthy, whether the man is well-balanced, whether the man is capable of giving life, of evangelising, whether the man is capable of forming a family and renouncing this in order to follow Jesus*".

63. In preparing for the theological or configuration stage, and leading to a definitive choice for priesthood, this stage allows for systematic work on the personality of the seminarian, in openness to the Holy Spirit. For priestly formation the importance of human formation cannot be sufficiently emphasised. Indeed, the holiness of a priest is built upon it and depends, in large part, upon the authenticity and maturity of his humanity. The lack of a well structured and balanced personality is a serious and objective hindrance to the continuation of formation for the priesthood.

For this reason, seminarians should become accustomed to training their character, they should grow in their strength of spirit and, generally speaking, they should learn human virtues, such as "*sincerity of mind, a constant concern for justice, fidelity to one's promises, refinement in manners, modesty in speech coupled with charity*".[96] This will make them a living reflection of the humanity of Jesus and a bridge that unites people with God. In order to attain the solid physical, psycho-affective and social maturity required of a pastor, it is useful to have recourse to physical exercise and sports, along with preparation for a well-balanced lifestyle. As well as the irreplaceable accompaniment of the formators and the Spiritual Director, specific psychological accompaniment could be of help in some cases, to integrate the fundamental elements of the personality.

This process of formation is intended to educate the person in the truth of his being, in freedom and in self-control. It is meant to overcome all kinds of individualism, and to foster the sincere gift of self, opening him to generous dedication to others.

64. Growth in human maturity is assisted and brought about by divine grace, which gives direction to the growth of the spiritual life. This in turn helps the seminarian to live in the presence of God in an attitude of prayer, and it is based on his personal relationship with Christ, that consolidates the identity of discipleship.

65. This is a transformative journey that involves the whole community. Through the specific role of the formators and, in a special way, the Spiritual Director, a pedagogical itinerary is proposed, which sustains the

---

[96] *Optatam Totius*, n. 11: *AAS* 58 (1966), 720.

candidate in the process of growth, helping him to become aware of his own poverty and, at the same time, of his need for the grace of God and fraternal correction.

66. The duration of this stage, which must not be less than two years, should be sufficient to attain its own proper objectives and, at the same time, to acquire the necessary knowledge of philosophy and of the human sciences. It must be valued properly in its own right and understood with regard to its specific aims, and not simply as an "obligatory step" needed to reach theological studies.

67. At the end of the stage of philosophical studies, or discipleship, having reached an adequate inner freedom and maturity, the seminarian should be possessed of the means necessary to begin that journey, with serenity and joy. This will lead him to a greater configuration to Christ in the vocation to ordained ministry. Indeed, after this stage, it will be possible to admit the seminarian among the candidates for Orders (*petitio* or candidacy, etc.), when it is deemed that his intention, marked by the required qualities, has reached sufficient maturity.[97] For her part, in accepting the seminarian who offers himself, the Church chooses him and calls him so that he may prepare to receive Holy Orders in the future. Since it presupposes a responsible decision on the part of the seminarian, admission among the candidates for Orders is an invitation for him to continue with his formation, in configuring himself to Christ the Shepherd, through a formal recognition on the part of the Church.

a.3. The Stage of Theological Studies (or Configuration)

68. *The concept of configuration.* The whole life of a priest, from the first moment of his calling, is, as already stated, one of continuous formation. It is the life of a disciple of Jesus, docile to the action of the Holy Spirit, for the service of the Church. The pedagogy of initial formation, in the first years in seminary, was aimed above all at leading the candidate to enter into the *sequela Christi*. At the conclusion of that stage, the so-called discipleship stage, formation then concentrates on the configuration of the

---

[97] Cf. PAUL VI, Apostolic Letter *Ad Pascendum* (15 August 1972), I, a) and c): *AAS* 64 (1972), 538-539.

seminarian to Christ, Shepherd and Servant, so that, united to him, he can make his life a gift of self to others.

This configuration demands that the seminarian enter profoundly into the contemplation of the person of Jesus Christ, the beloved Son of the Father, sent as Shepherd of the People of God. It will make the relationship with Christ more intimate and personal and, at the same time, will lead to an awareness and an assumption of priestly identity.

69. The stage of theological studies, or of configuration, is aimed above all at the spiritual formation proper to the priest. Gradual configuration to Christ becomes an experience which causes the sentiments and attitudes of the Son of God to arise in the life of the disciple. At the same time, it introduces the seminarian to an appreciation of the life of a priest, inspired by the desire and sustained by the capacity to offer himself for the pastoral care of the People of God. This stage allows the gradual grounding of the seminarian in the likeness of the Good Shepherd, who knows his sheep, gives his life for them[98] and seeks out the ones that have wandered from the fold (cf. *Jn* 10:14-17).

The content of this stage is demanding and requires a great deal of commitment. It asks for a constant responsibility in living the cardinal and theological virtues and the evangelical counsels.[99] It demands a docility to the action of God through the promptings of Holy Spirit, according to an authentically priestly and missionary mindset. It also calls for a gradual rereading of one's own personal history in the light of pastoral charity, which animates, forms and motivates the life of the priest.[100]

70. The special commitment that characterises configuration to Christ, Servant and Shepherd, can correspond to the theological stage, without this

---

[98] *Directory for the Ministry and Life of Priests*, n. 8: "*It can therefore be said that the configuration to Christ through sacramental consecration defines the priest within the People of God, making him participate in his own way in the sanctifying, magisterial and pastoral power of Jesus Christ himself, Head and Pastor of the Church. Becoming increasingly like unto Christ, the priest is - thanks to him, and to himself - a co-worker in the salvation of his brethren: it is no longer he who loves and exists, but Christ in him (cf. Gal 2:20)*".

[99] Cf. *Pastores Dabo Vobis*, n. 27: *AAS* 84 (1992), 710.

[100] Cf. *ibid*, n. 23: *AAS* 84 (1992), 691-694.

necessarily exhausting its dynamism or its content. Concretely, a fruitful and harmonious interaction should be achieved between human and spiritual maturity, between the life of prayer and theological understanding.

71. With a view to service in a particular Church, seminarians are called to acquire the spirituality of a diocesan priest, which is characterised by selfless dedication to the ecclesiastical circumscription to which they belong, or to the one in which they will in fact exercise the ministry, for the diocesan priest is the shepherd and servant of all in a specific context (cf. *1 Cor* 9:19). As a bond with the local Church, belonging to a diocese specifically concerns the secular clergy, but it also pertains to all the priests who exercise the ministry there, without prejudice to the proper charism of each. This also means conforming one's own way of thinking and working in communion with the bishop and brother priests, for the good of a portion of the People of God.[101]

This indispensable love for the diocese can be enriched by other charisms, brought about by the action of the Holy Spirit. In the same way, the gift of priesthood received in Holy Orders includes a commitment to the Universal Church and, because of that, it is open to the mission of salvation addressed to all people, even to the ends of the earth (cf. *Acts* 1:8).[102]

72. During this stage, the ministries of lector and acolyte will be conferred upon seminarians, according to the maturing of each individual candidate and at an appropriate moment in the formation programme. They will then be able to exercise these ministries for a suitable period of time, and prepare themselves better for their future service of Word and Altar.[103] Lectorate "challenges" the seminarian to allow himself to be transformed

---

[101] FRANCIS, *Address to the Priests of the Diocese of Caserta* (26 July 2014): *L'Osservatore Romano* 171 (28-29 July 2014), 5: "*the spirituality of the diocesan priest is to be open to diocesan life* [...] *It means a relationship with the bishop, which must be realised and must grow continuously* [...] *Secondly, the diocesan life involves a relationship with the other priests, with all the presbytery. There is no spirituality of the diocesan priest without these two relationships: with the bishop and with the presbyter. And they are needed*".

[102] Cf. *Presbyterorum Ordinis*, n. 10: *AAS* 58 (1966), 1007-1008; *Pastores Dabo Vobis*, n. 17: *AAS* 84 (1992), 682-684.

[103] Cf. PAUL VI, Apostolic Letter *Ministeria Quaedam* (15 August 1972), V-VI: *AAS* 64 (1972), 532-533.

by the Word of God, the object of his prayer and study. The conferral of the ministry of acolyte implies a deeper participation in the mystery of Christ, who gives himself and is present in the Eucharist, in the assembly and in his brothers and sisters.

For these reasons, the two ministries, accompanied by a suitable spiritual preparation, allow the demands of the *configuration stage* to be lived more intensely. During this stage, therefore, it is fitting for lectors and acolytes to be offered concrete ways of exercising the ministries received, not only in the liturgical environment, but also in catechesis, evangelisation, and the service of their neighbour.

In any case, the right kind of accompaniment may reveal that the call which the young man believed that he had received, although recognised during the first stage, was not truly a vocation to the ministerial priesthood. Alternatively, it may not have been cultivated sufficiently. In either case, the seminarian should interrupt the journey of formation towards priestly ordination, either on his own initiative or following an authoritative intervention on the part of the formators.

73. The stage of theological studies, or of configuration, is nevertheless oriented towards the conferral of Holy Orders. At the conclusion of this stage, or during the following one, if he has been judged suitable by the bishop, after having heard the formators, the seminarian will petition to receive diaconal ordination. With diaconal ordination he will enter the clerical state, with its associated rights and duties, and will be incardinated "*either in a particular Church or personal prelature, or in an institute of consecrated life or society*"[104], or in an Association or Ordinariate with the faculty to incardinate.

a.4. The Pastoral Stage (or Vocational Synthesis)

74. The pastoral stage, or vocational synthesis, is the time from leaving the seminary until the subsequent priestly ordination, which obviously is brought about by conferral of the diaconate. This stage has a twofold purpose: on the one hand it is about being inducted into the pastoral life, with a gradual assumption of responsibilities in a spirit of service; on the other hand it is about making an suitable preparation, with the help

---

[104] C.I.C., can. 265.

of a specific accompaniment, in view of priesthood. During this stage, the candidate is asked to declare freely, consciously and definitively his intention to be a priest, having received diaconal ordination.[105]

75. In this regard, there are a great variety of experiences in the particular Churches, and it belongs to the Conferences of Bishops to determine the formative programmes in preparation for diaconal and priestly ordination. This stage will normally take place outside of the seminary building, at least for a significant period of time. This period, which will normally be lived in the service of a community, can make a great impact on the personality of the candidate. Consequently, it is recommended that the pastor [*parochus*], or whichever person is responsible for the pastoral setting that receives the seminarian, should be aware of the formative task entrusted to him, and should accompany him in his gradual entry to pastoral ministry.

76. The Ordinary, by mutual agreement with the Rector of the seminary where the seminarian has received his formation, and taking account of the needs of the presbyterate and the opportunities for formation available, shall assign each seminarian to a community where he will offer his pastoral service.[106] The duration of this stage of formation varies, and depends on the maturity and suitability of the candidate. Nonetheless, at least the times canonically established between the reception of the diaconate and of the presbyterate must be respected.[107]

77. *Diaconal and presbyteral ordination*. At the conclusion of the cycle of seminary formation, the formators must help the candidate to accept with docility the decision the bishop has made in his regard.[108]

---

[105] Cf. *Optatam Totius*, n. 12: *AAS* 58 (1966), 721.

[106] Cf. *ibid.*, n. 21: *AAS* 58 (1966), 726.

[107] Cf. C.I.C., cann. 1031, §1 and 1032, §2.

[108] Cf. BENEDICT XVI, Post-Synodal Apostolic Exhortation *Sacramentum Caritatis* (22 February 2007), n. 25: *AAS* 99 (2007), 125-126.

Those who receive Holy Orders need a suitable time of preparation, especially of a spiritual nature.[109] A spirit of prayer, founded on a relationship with the person of Jesus, and an encounter with exemplary models of priesthood, should accompany an attentive reflection on the ordination rites which, in the prayers and liturgical actions, synthesise and express the profound meaning of the sacrament of Orders in the Church.

78. The family of the candidate and the whole parish community should also experience an intense period of preparation. The specific formative programmes for diaconate and for priesthood, however, should be clearly distinguished, since they are two very different moments. Thus, unless serious reasons suggest otherwise, it will not be preferable to join in one celebration both diaconal ordination (transitional or permanent) and presbyteral ordination, so as to give each moment the attention it deserves, and to help the understanding of the faithful.

79. *Connection to ongoing formation.* Beginning with presbyteral ordination, the formation process continues within the family of the presbyterate. It belongs to the bishop, with the help of his assistants, to lead priests into the dynamic of ongoing formation.[110]

(B) ONGOING FORMATION

80. The term "ongoing formation"[111] is a reminder that the one experience of discipleship of those called to priesthood is never interrupted. The priest not only "learns to know Christ" but, under the action of the Holy Spirit, he finds himself within a process of gradual and continuous configuration

---

[109] Cf. C.I.C., can. 1039.

[110] Cf. *Apostolorum Successores*, n. 83: *Enchiridion Vaticanum* 22 (2006), 1764-1766.

[111] Over the course of time, the concept of ongoing formation has been deepened both in society and in the Church. An important moment in this process was the *Letter to Priests* (especially no. 10) issued by John Paul II on 8 April 1979: *Insegnamenti* II (1979), 857-859: "we must all be converted anew every day. We know that this is a fundamental exigency of the Gospel, addressed to everyone (cf. Mt 4:17; Mk 1:15), and all the more do we have to consider it as addressed to us [...] We must link prayer with continuous work upon ourselves: this is the formatio permanens [...] this formation must be both interior, that is to say directed towards the deepening of the priest's spiritual life, and must also be pastoral and intellectual (philosophical and theological)". For a general overview and synthesis on this point, see *General Directory for the Ministry and Life of Priests*, nn. 87-115.

to him, in his being and his acting, which constantly challenges the person to inner growth.[112]

One must constantly feed the "fire" that gives light and warmth to the exercise of the ministry, remembering that, *"the heart and form of the priest's ongoing formation is pastoral charity"*.[113]

81. Ongoing formation is intended to ensure fidelity to the priestly ministry in a continuing journey of conversion, in order to rekindle the gift received at ordination.[114] This journey is the natural continuation of the process of building up priestly identity begun in seminary and accomplished sacramentally in priestly ordination, in view of a pastoral service that causes it to mature over time.[115]

82. It is important that the faithful should be able to encounter priests who are suitably mature and formed. Indeed, *"corresponding to this serious duty is a precise right on the part of the faithful, who positively feel the effects of the good formation and holiness of their priests"*.[116] Ongoing formation must be concrete, that is to say incarnate in priestly reality, so that all priests can undertake it effectively; after all, it is the priest himself who is principally and primarily responsible for his own ongoing formation.[117]

Priestly fraternity is the first setting in which ongoing formation is takes place. It is desirable that this formation be promoted in each diocese by a priest or group of priests, specifically prepared for it and officially appointed to assist in ongoing formation. The different age groups and particular circumstances of the brethren should be taken into consideration.[118]

---

[112] Cf. FRANCIS, *Address to the Plenary of the Congregation for the Clergy* (3 October 2014): *L'Osservatore Romano* 226 (4 October 2014), 8.
[113] *Pastores Dabo Vobis*, n. 70: *AAS* 84 (1992), 781.
[114] Cf. *ibid.*: *AAS* 84 (1992), 778-782.
[115] Cf. *ibid.*, n. 71: *AAS* 84 (1992), 782-783.
[116] *Directory for the Ministry and Life of Priests*, n. 87.
[117] Cf. *Pastores Dabo Vobis*, n. 79: *AAS* 84 (1992), 796.
[118] Cf. *Directory for the Ministry and Life of Priests*, n. 108.

83. The first phase of this journey corresponds to the years immediately after priestly ordination. In this period, the priest acquires, through the exercise of the ministry, fidelity to the personal encounter with the Lord and to his own spiritual accompaniment, along with the openness to asking the advice of priests with more experience. Particularly significant is the capacity to establish relationships of cooperation and sharing with other priests of the same generation. It is desirable that accompaniment by confreres of exemplary life and pastoral zeal be promoted, so that they can help young priests to experience a cordial and active participation in the life of the entire diocesan presbyterate.

It is the bishop's responsibility to "*to ensure that newly ordained priests are not immersed in excessively burdensome or delicate situations, and that they are not assigned to destinations where they would be working far away from their confreres. In fact, it will be good to foster some opportune form of common life insofar as possible*".[119] It is good to set up a system of personal accompaniment of young priests, to promote and maintain the quality of their ministry, so that they can embrace their first pastoral challenges with enthusiasm. It is the pastor [*parochus*] above all who should assume responsibility for this, or whichever priest it is to whom the young priest has first been sent.

84. After some years of pastoral experience, new challenges for the ministry and life of the priest can easily emerge:

a. *The experience of one's own weakness*: conflicts that may remain in his personality can emerge and these need to be addressed. The experience of his own weakness can lead the priest to a greater humility and trust in the merciful action of the Lord - whose "strength is shown most fully in weakness" (cf. *2 Cor* 12:9) - as well as a generous understanding of others. The priest must not become isolated. Instead he should be supported and accompanied in spiritual and/or psychological areas. In every case, his relationship with his Spiritual Director will need to be deepened so as to draw positive lessons from the difficulties, learning to look truthfully at his own life and to understand it better in the light of the Gospel.

---
[119] *Ibid.*, n. 100.

b. *The risk of thinking of oneself simply as a dispenser of sacred things*: with the passage of time, the priest can acquire the idea that he is a mere community worker or a dispenser of sacred things[120], without the heart of a shepherd. As soon as he notices this, it will be important for the priest to sense the closeness of his confreres and to draw closer to them. Indeed, as Pope Francis has remarked, *"there is no need for [...] functionary priests who, while playing a role, seek their consolation far from him. Only one whose gaze is fixed on what is truly essential can renew his 'yes' to the gift received and, in life's various seasons, does not cease to make a gift of himself; only one who lets himself be conformed to the Good Shepherd finds unity, peace and strength in the obedience of service..."*.[121]

c. *The challenge of contemporary culture*: the appropriate involvement of the priestly ministry in the culture of today, with all the complex problems that it brings in its wake, requires openness in priests and that they remain up to date.[122] Above all, it requires that they remain firmly anchored to the four dimensions of formation: human, spiritual, intellectual and pastoral.

d. *The allure of power and riches*: this may take the form of attachment to a position, obsession with marking out space exclusively for oneself, careerism, emergence of hunger for power or the desire for wealth, with the consequent lack of openness to the will of God, to the needs of the people entrusted to his care, or to the requests of the bishop. Fraternal correction may help in such circumstances, or even a reproof or some other approach suggested by pastoral concern, unless the behaviour constitutes a delict that calls for the imposition of penalties.

e. *The challenge of celibacy*: how to live celibacy for the Kingdom in a context where new stimuli and the tensions of pastoral life, instead of

---

[120] Cf. *Pastores Dabo Vobis*, n. 72: *AAS* 84 (1992), 783-787.

[121] FRANCIS, *Letter to the Participants in the Extraordinary General Assembly of the Italian Episcopal Conference* (8 November 2014): *L'Osservatore Romano* 258 (12 November 2014), 7; cf. *Presbyterorum Ordinis*, n. 14: *AAS* 58 (1966), 1013-1014.

[122] Cf. *Pastores Dabo Vobis*, n. 78: *AAS* 84 (1992), 795-796.

assisting the growth and maturing of the person, can lead to emotional regression. Influenced by strong social pressures, this can lead to giving undue priority to one's own needs and seeking out forms of compensatory behaviour, thus hampering priestly fatherhood and pastoral charity.

f. *Total dedication to one's ministry*: with the passage of time, tiredness, natural physical weaknesses, and the first manifestations of frail health, conflicts, disappointments over pastoral expectations, the burden of routine, the fatigue induced by change, and other socio-cultural elements can dampen apostolic zeal and generosity in giving oneself to the pastoral ministry.

85. At any age, a priest may require help due to some infirmity. Elderly and ailing priests offer to the Christian community, and to the presbyterate, their own witness and are an effective and eloquent sign of a life given to the Lord. It is important that they continue to feel themselves an active part of the presbyterate and of diocesan life, especially through frequent visits from and the solicitous closeness of their confreres.

86. Initiatives for the support of priests, born out of a concern for priests who are exercising the ministry in the same geographical area, in the same pastoral environment, or who are involved in the same project, are also praiseworthy.

87. Sacramental fraternity is a valuable help for the ongoing formation of priests. Indeed, the journey of discipleship requires constant growth in charity, which is the synthesis of *"priestly perfection"*.[123] However, this cannot be achieved in isolation, since priests form one presbyterate whose unity is made up of *"special bonds of apostolic charity, ministry and brotherhood"*.[124] Thus, the *"intimate sacramental fraternity"*[125] of priests is the first manifestation of charity, as well as the first place in which it can grow. All this can be achieved by the help of the Holy Spirit, and not without a personal spiritual struggle to purify oneself of all forms of individualism.

---

[123] *Presbyterorum Ordinis*, n. 14: *AAS* 58 (1966), 1013.
[124] *Ibid.*, n. 8: *AAS* 58 (1966), 1004.
[125] *Ibid.*: *AAS* 58 (1966), 1003.

88. Among those ways that can give concrete expression to sacramental fraternity, some in particular should be encouraged from the time of initial formation:

a. *Fraternal meetings*: some priests organise *fraternal meetings* for prayer, perhaps by reading the Word of God together in the form of *lectio divina*, developing their understanding of some theological or pastoral theme, sharing a ministerial endeavour, helping one another or simply spending some time together. These meetings in their various forms are the simplest and most common expression of priestly fraternity. In any case, it is strongly desirable to promote them.

b. *Spiritual Direction and confession*: sacramental fraternity becomes a particularly valuable help when it takes the form of *spiritual direction* and confession, which priests ask one another to provide. Maintaining a regular schedule in this type of meeting helps to keep alive the *"striving for spiritual perfection on which, above all, the effectiveness of their ministry depends"*.[126] It is particularly in moments of difficulty that priests will find in their Spiritual Director a brother, who can help them to discern the source of their difficulties, and put adequate means in place to address them.

c. *Retreats*: these are of fundamental importance in the life of the priest, since they lead to a personal encounter with the Lord in silence and recollection. They are a privileged time of personal and apostolic discernment, for a gradual and profound review of one's life. When offered as a group experience for priests, they can favour a wider participation and the strengthening of fraternal communion.

d. *A common table*: when they share meals, priests come to know one another, to listen to and to appreciate one another. This also gives them the opportunity for worthwhile friendly exchanges.

---

[126] BENEDICT XVI, *Address to Participants in the Plenary of the Congregation for the Clergy* (16 March 2009): *Insegnamenti* V/1 (2009), 392.

e. *Common Life*: some priests share a common life as a personal initiative, out of pastoral necessity, or through custom or local arrangements.[127] Sharing the same house becomes a true "common life" through community prayer, meditation on the Word of God and other opportunities for ongoing formation. Moreover, this arrangement allows for a sharing of ideas about pastoral endeavours of each priest. A common life also seeks to support the emotional and spiritual balance of those involved, and can encourage communion with the bishop. It will be necessary to ensure that forms of common life remain open to the entire presbyterate and to the pastoral needs of the diocese.

f. *Priestly Associations*: these are meant to encourage the unity of the priests among themselves, with the rest of the presbyterate and with the bishop.[128] Members of various associations recognised by the Church find fraternal support there, which priests feel they need, so as to progress on the journey to holiness and to be sustained in their pastoral endeavours.[129] Some priests also belong to new ecclesial movements, where they find an atmosphere of communion and renewed missionary zeal. Others still live a personal consecration within Secular Institutes *"which have as their characteristic feature their being diocesan"*[130], without necessarily being incardinated within the Institute.

---

[127] Cf. C.I.C., can. 280; *Directory for the Ministry and Life of Priests*, n. 38.
[128] Cf. C.I.C., can. 278, §§ 1-2.
[129] Cf. *Directory for the Ministry and Life of Priests*, n. 106.
[130] *Pastores Dabo Vobis*, n. 81: *AAS* 84 (1992), 799.

V. DIMENSIONS OF FORMATION

(A) INTEGRATING THE DIMENSIONS OF FORMATION

89. According to the Apostolic Exhortation *Pastores Dabo Vobis*[131], there are four dimensions that interact simultaneously in the *iter* of formation and in the life of ordained ministers: the human dimension, which represents the "necessary and dynamic foundation" of all priestly life; the spiritual dimension, which helps to shape the quality of priestly ministry; the intellectual dimension, which provides the rational tools needed in order to understand the values that belong to being a pastor, to make them incarnate in daily life, and to transmit the content of the faith appropriately; the pastoral dimension, which makes possible a responsible and fruitful ecclesial service.

Each of the dimensions of formation is aimed at "transforming" or "assimilating" the heart in the image of the heart of Christ[132], who was sent by the Father to fulfil his loving plan. He was moved when faced with human suffering (cf. *Mt* 9:35-36), he went to seek out the lost sheep (cf. *Mt* 18:12-14), even to offering his life for them (cf. *Jn* 10:11). He came not to be served but to serve (cf. *Mt* 20:24-28). As the Second Vatican Council indicates[133], the entire process of formation in preparation for priestly ministry, in fact, has as its aim the preparation of seminarians to *"enter into communion with the charity of Christ the Good Shepherd"*.[134]

90. By the sacrament of Orders, the seminarian will be called to gather into one and to preside over the People of God, as a leader who supports and promotes the cooperation of all the faithful. Priestly formation must therefore take place within an atmosphere of community, which is able to encourage those attitudes that are proper and of practical value for the life and ministry of a priest.[135]

---

[131] Cf. *Pastores Dabo Vobis*, nn. 43-59: *AAS* 84 (1992), 731-762.

[132] Cf. *Optatam Totius*, n. 4: *AAS* 58 (1966), 716; *Pastores Dabo Vobis*, n. 57: *AAS* 84 (1992), 757-759.

[133] Cf. *Optatam Totius* nn. 4 and 19: *AAS* 58 (1966), 716 and 725-726

[134] *Pastores Dabo Vobis*, n. 57: *AAS* 84 (1992), 757-758.

[135] *Ibid.*, n. 65: *AAS* 84 (1992), 770: *"the Church as such is the communal subject which has the grace and responsibility to accompany those whom the Lord calls to become his ministers in the priesthood"*.

Community life in the seminary is the most suitable context for preparing seminarians for true priestly fraternity. It is the environment in which the aforementioned dimensions come together and interact, and where they attain to mutual harmony and integration. Certain formative instruments should be adopted for community formation and for a better knowledge of the individual seminarians, such as: sincere and open communication, exchange, review of life, fraternal correction, and community programmes.

The community forms the seedbed of a priestly vocation, since the seminarian emerges from it, in order to be sent back to serve it after ordination. The seminarian to begin with, and later the priest, must have a living bond with the community. It is the thread that binds together and harmonises the four dimensions of formation.

91. The Christian community is brought together by the Spirit in order to be sent out on mission. Thus the missionary impulse and its concrete manifestation belong to the entire People of God[136], which must always be *"going forth"*[137], since *"the Gospel joy which enlivens the community of disciples is a missionary joy"*.[138] This missionary drive concerns those called to the ministerial priesthood even more particularly, as it is the goal and the horizon of all formation. Mission is another thread that binds (cf. *Mk* 3:13-14), animates and gives life to the dimensions already mentioned. It allows the priest, who has been formed humanly, intellectually, spiritually and pastorally, to live his ministry fully, since he is *"called to have a missionary spirit, that is to say a truly 'catholic' spirit, which, beginning from Christ, reaches out to all so that 'they may be saved and reach full knowledge of the truth' (1 Tm 2:4)"*.[139]

92. The concept of integral formation is of the greatest importance, since it is the whole person, with all that he is and all that he possesses, who will be at the Lord's service in the Christian community. The one called is an "integral subject", namely someone who has been previously chosen

---

[136] Cf. *Evangelii Gaudium*, nn. 119-121: *AAS* 105 (2013), 1069-1071.

[137] *Ibid.*, n. 20: *AAS* 105 (2013), 1028.

[138] *Ibid.*, n. 21: *AAS* 105 (2013), 1028.

[139] *Directory for the Ministry and Life of Priests*, n. 16.

to attain a sound interior life, without divisions or contradictions. It is necessary to adopt an integrated pedagogical model in order to reach this objective: a journey that allows the formative community to cooperate with the action of the Holy Spirit, ensuring a proper balance between the different dimensions of formation.

For this reason, it is necessary to be vigilant, lest overly simplistic or erroneous visions of the priesthood should find their way into the *iter* of formation. Formators should be attentive in discerning whether there is a merely formal and external respect given to the formation demands placed upon those entrusted to their care. Such an attitude would not help their integral growth but rather would make them accustomed, more or less unconsciously, to a purely "servile and self-serving" obedience.

(B) THE HUMAN DIMENSION

93. The divine call engages and involves the "concrete" human person. Formation for the priesthood must necessarily provide adequate means to allow for maturation in view of an authentic exercise of the priestly ministry. To that end, the seminarian is called upon to develop his personality, having Christ, the perfect man, as his model and source.

The criteria of suitability for ordained ministers received ample reflection in the New Testament.[140] This illustrates the extent to which aspects relating to the human dimension were highlighted from the very beginning. The Church Fathers developed and practised the care or "therapy" of the man of faith called to apostolic service, for they were convinced of the profound need for maturation that remains in everyone.[141] A correct and harmonious spirituality demands a well-structured humanity; indeed, as St Thomas Aquinas reminds us, "*grace builds upon nature*"[142], it does not supplant nature, but perfects it.[143] Therefore, it is necessary to cultivate humility, courage, common sense, magnanimity, right judgement and discretion, tolerance and transparency, love of truth and honesty.

---

[140] For example, cf. *Mt* 28:20; *1 Pt* 5:1-4; *Tit* 1:5-9.

[141] For example, one can think of GREGORY NAZIANZEN, *Oratio II*: PG 35, 27.

[142] THOMAS AQUINAS, *Summa Theologiae*, I, q. 2, a. 2 ad 1.

[143] Cf. *ibid.*, I, q. 1, a. 8 ad 2.

94. Human formation, being the foundation of all priestly formation[144], promotes the integral growth of the person and allows the integration of all its dimensions. Physically, this means an interest in health, nutrition, physical activity, and rest; psychologically it focuses on the constitution of a stable personality, characterised by emotional balance, self-control and a well integrated sexuality. In the moral sphere, it is connected to the requirement that the individual arrive gradually at a well-formed conscience. This means that he will become a responsible person able to make the right decisions, gifted with right judgement and able to have an objective perception of persons and events. Such a perspective should bring the seminarian to a balanced sense of self-respect, leading him to be aware of his own talents and learning how to place them at the service of the People of God. The aesthetic sense should also be cultivated in human formation, by offering opportunities for an appreciation of various modes of artistic expression, cultivating in him the "sense of beauty". He ought to be aware of the social environment, and be helped to improve his capacity for social interaction, so that he can contribute to building up the community in which he lives.

In order for this training to be fruitful, it is important that every seminarian be aware of his own life history, and be ready to share it with his formators. This would include especially his experience of childhood and adolescence, the influence that his family and his relatives have exercised upon him, his ability to establish mature and well balanced interpersonal relationships, or his lack thereof, and his ability to handle positively moments of solitude. Such information will be helpful for choosing the most fitting pedagogical means, both for an assessment of the journey thus far and for a better understanding of any moments of regression or of difficulty.

95. A sign of the harmonious development of the personality of seminarians is a mature capacity for relations with men and women of various ages and social conditions. It would be fitting to take into consideration the relationship between the seminarian and women, as addressed in Magisterial documents where we read that it affects *"the seminarian not only in the sphere of his personal life, but also with a view to his future pastoral activity"*.[145]

---

[144] Cf. *Pastores Dabo Vobis*, n. 43: *AAS* 84 (1992), 731-732.

[145] *A Guide to Formation in Priestly Celibacy*, n. 60.

The first environment in which someone comes to be acquainted with and appreciate women is obviously within the family. The presence of a woman there accompanies the entire formative journey and constitutes, from infancy onwards, a positive contribution to integral growth. Another significant contribution comes from the various women who, by the witness of their lives, give an example of prayer and pastoral service, a spirit of sacrifice and self-denial, of care and tender closeness to their neighbour. A similar reflection could be made about the witness given by the presence of consecrated women.

This understanding and this familiarity with the feminine, so present in parishes and many ecclesial contexts, are beneficial and essential to the human and spiritual formation of the seminarian, and should always be seen in a positive light. As John Paul II remarked: *"it is thus my hope [...] that you will reflect carefully on what it means to speak of the 'genius of women', not only in order to be able to see in this phrase a specific part of God's plan which needs to be accepted and appreciated, but also in order to let this genius be more fully expressed in the life of society as a whole, as well as in the life of the Church"*.[146]

96. The seminarian also becomes capable of self-determination and living with responsibility through an awareness of his own weakness, which is always present in his personality. Formators, confessors, spiritual directors and the seminarians themselves should be aware that moments of crisis, if adequately understood and addressed, with a willingness to learn from life, can and must become occasions of conversion and renewal. These moments will lead the seminarian to question himself critically about the journey so far, about his current condition, about his choices and about his future.

97. Human formation is a necessary element for evangelisation, since the proclamation of the Gospel takes place through the person and is mediated by his humanity. *"You will be my witnesses [...] to the ends of the earth"* (cf. *Acts* 1:8). Modern day reality obliges us to think about these words of Jesus in a new way, because *"the ends of the earth"* have expanded

---

[146] JOHN PAUL II, *Letter to Women* (29 June 1995), n. 10: *Insegnamenti* XVIII/1 (1995), 1879; cf. *A Guide to Formation in Priestly Celibacy*, n. 59.

through the mass media and social networks. It is "*a new 'agora', an open public square in which people share ideas, information and opinions, and in which new relationships and forms of community can come into being*"[147], an arena from which the pastors of the future cannot remain aloof, either during their formation or their future ministry.

From that point of view, the use of the media and ease with the digital world are an integral part of the development of the personality of the seminarian, because, "*using new communication technologies, priests can introduce people to the life of the Church and help our contemporaries to discover the face of Christ. They will best achieve this aim if they learn, from the time of their formation, how to use these technologies in a competent and appropriate way, shaped by sound theological insights and reflecting a strong priestly spirituality grounded in constant dialogue with the Lord*".[148]

98. The Church, in virtue of the mandate received from Christ, looks confidently at the possibilities offered by the digital world for evangelisation.[149] There are new "places" through which many are moving daily, "digital peripheries" which should not be deprived of the possibility of an authentic culture of encounter in the name of Jesus, to build up one People of God: "*the media can help us to feel closer to one another, creating a sense of the unity of the human family which can in turn inspire solidarity and serious efforts to ensure a more dignified life for all. Good communication helps us to grow closer, to know one another better, and ultimately, to grow in unity*".[150]

99. Those who begin the seminary journey are, for the most part, already naturally quite adept and immersed in the digital world and its instruments.

---

[147] BENEDICT XVI, *Message for the XLVII World Communications Day* (12 May 2013): *AAS* 105 (2013), 181.

[148] ID., *Message for the XLIV World Communications Day* (16 May 2010): *AAS* 102 (2010), 115-116.

[149] FRANCIS, *Message for the XLVIII World Communications Day* (1 June 2014): *AAS* 106 (2014), 115: "*Keeping the doors of our churches open also means keeping them open in the digital environment so that people, whatever their situation in life, can enter, and so that the Gospel can go out to reach everyone*".

[150] *Ibid.*: *AAS* 106 (2014), 113.

It is necessary to pay prudent attention to the inevitable risks that come with frequenting the digital world, including various forms of addiction, which can be addressed with suitable spiritual and psychological supports. It is fitting for seminarians to grow in this context, keeping in mind that the seminary is a school of humanity and faith, so that their conformation to Christ can grow. He brings himself close to all humanity, even those who are far off: *"may the image of the Good Samaritan who tended to the wounds of the injured man by pouring oil and wine over them be our inspiration. Let our communication be a balm which relieves pain and a fine wine which gladdens hearts. May the light we bring to others not be the result of cosmetics or special effects, but rather of our being loving and merciful 'neighbours' to those wounded and left on the side of the road"*.[151]

100. Social networks should be integrated into the daily life of the seminary community in a particular way (by a use that is vigilant, but also serene and positive). They should be experienced as places that offer new possibilities from the point of view of interpersonal relationships, of encounter with others, of engagement with one's neighbour, of the witness of faith. These may all be viewed from the perspective of formative growth, which cannot fail to take into consideration every place in which relationships are formed and in which we find ourselves living.

(C) THE SPIRITUAL DIMENSION

101. Spiritual formation is directed at nourishing and sustaining communion with God and with our brothers and sisters, in the friendship of Jesus the Good Shepherd, and with an attitude of docility to the Holy Spirit.[152] This intimate relationship forms the heart of the seminarian in that generous and sacrificial love that marks the beginning of pastoral charity.

102. The heart of spiritual formation is personal union with Christ, which is born of, and nourished in, a particular way by prolonged and silent prayer.[153] By prayer, listening to the Word, devout participation in the

---

[151] *Ibid.*: AAS 106 (2014), 116.
[152] Cf. *Presbyterorum Ordinis*, n. 12: AAS 58 (1966), 1009-1011.
[153] Cf. *Catechism of the Catholic Church*, nn. 2709-2719.

sacraments, in the liturgy and in community life, the seminarian fortifies his personal union with God after the example of Christ, who had, as his programme of life, to do the will of his Father (cf. *Jn* 4:34). In the journey of formation, the liturgical year offers the pedagogical mystagogy of the Church, allowing its spirituality to be absorbed by interiorising the scriptural texts and liturgical prayers.[154]

103. We must always remember that, *"ignorance of the Scriptures is ignorance of Christ"*.[155] Therefore, a relationship with the Word of God holds a pre-eminent place in the process of spiritual growth.[156] Before it is ever preached, the Word must be welcomed in the depth of the heart[157], *"above all in the context of the 'new evangelisation' to which the Church is called today"*.[158] The new evangelisation is the continuous point of reference for the life of discipleship and spiritual configuration to Christ the Good Shepherd. Seminarians need to be introduced gradually to the knowledge of the Word of God, through the method known as *lectio divina*.[159] A profound daily meditation[160], practised with fidelity and diligence, in which study and prayer come together in a reciprocal fruitfulness, will ensure an integral approach[161] to both the Old and New Testaments.

---

[154] *"The entire liturgical year, in regard not only to the liturgical celebration but to life itself, should be a spiritual journey to participate intimately in the mystery of Christ"*: SACRED CONGREGATION FOR CATHOLIC EDUCATION, Instruction *on Liturgical Formation in Seminaries* (3 June 1979), n. 32: *Enchiridion Vaticanum* 6 (2001), 1590.

[155] JEROME, *Commentarii in Isaiam*, Prologus: CCL 73, 1.

[156] BENEDICT XVI, Post-Synodal Apostolic Exhortation *Verbum Domini* (30 September 2010), n. 82: *AAS* 102 (2010), 753: *"Those aspiring to the ministerial priesthood are called to a profound personal relationship with God's word, particularly in lectio divina, so that this relationship will in turn nurture their vocation: it is in the light and strength of God's word that one's specific vocation can be discerned and appreciated, loved and followed, and one's proper mission carried out, by nourishing the heart with thoughts of God, so that faith, as our response to the word, may become a new criterion for judging and evaluating persons and things, events and issues"*.

[157] Cf. ORIGEN, *Homilia in Lucam*, XXXII, 2: PG 13, 1884.

[158] *Pastores Dabo Vobis*, n. 47: *AAS* 84 (1992), 741.

[159] Cf. *ibid.*, n. 47: *AAS* 84 (1992), 740-742; *Verbum Domini*, nn. 86-87: *AAS* 102 (2010), 757-760.

[160] Cf. SECOND VATICAN ECUMENICAL COUNCIL, Dogmatic Constitution on Divine Revelation *Dei Verbum* (18 November 1965), n. 21: *AAS* 58 (1966), 828.

[161] Cf. *Verbum Domini*, n. 82: *AAS* 102 (2010), 753-754.

104. In virtue of their necessary conformation to Christ, *"candidates for ordination must, above all, be formed in a truly living faith in the Eucharist"*[162], in view of what they shall live after priestly ordination. Participation in the daily celebration of the Eucharist, which naturally flows into Eucharistic adoration[163], should permeate the life of the seminarian in such a way that a constant union with the Lord may mature.[164]

105. The Liturgy of the Hours cannot be lacking in the prayer life of a priest, and it is a true "school of prayer" for seminarians too.[165] Becoming gradually accustomed to the prayer of the Church through the Divine Office, they learn to taste its richness and beauty.[166]

106. Regular and frequent celebration of the sacrament of Penance, for which one should prepare by a daily examination of conscience, becomes, for the seminarian, an occasion to recognise with humility his own frailties and sins and, above all, to understand and experience the joy of feeling loved and forgiven by the Lord. Moreover, *"from it flows the sense of asceticism and interior discipline, a spirit of sacrifice and self-denial, the acceptance of hard work and of the cross"*.[167]

107. Spiritual direction is a privileged means for the integral growth of the person. The Spiritual Director is to be chosen with complete freedom by the seminarians from among the priests duly designated by the bishop.[168] This freedom will only be authentic when the seminarian opens himself

---

[162] JOHN PAUL II, *Angelus* (1 July 1990), n. 2: *Insegnamenti* XIII/2 (1990), 7. cf. C.I.C, can. 246, § 1.

[163] Cf. *Sacramentum Caritatis*, nn. 66-67: *AAS* 99 (2007), 155-156; AUGUSTINE, *Enarrationes in Psalmos*, 98, 9: CCL 39, 1385.

[164] *Pastores Dabo vobis*, n. 48: *AAS* 84 (1992), 743: *"They should, moreover, be trained to consider the Eucharistic celebration as the essential moment of their day, in which they will take an active part and at which they will never be satisfied with a merely habitual attendance"*.

[165] Cf. Instruction on *Liturgical Formation in Seminaries*, nn. 28-31: *Enchiridion Vaticanum* 6 (2001), 1583-1588; C.I.C., can. 276, § 2, n. 3.

[166] Cf. *Pastores Dabo Vobis*, n. 26: *AAS* 84 (1992), 697-700; cf. also Instruction *on Liturgical Formation in Seminaries*, n. 31: *Enchiridion Vaticanum* 6 (2001), 1587-1588.

[167] *Pastores Dabo Vobis*, n. 48: *AAS* 84 (1992), 744.

[168] Cf. C.I.C., can. 239, § 2.

up with sincerity, trust and docility. Meetings with the Spiritual Director must not be merely occasional, but scheduled and regular. Indeed, the quality of spiritual accompaniment is important for the very effectiveness of the whole process of formation.

Seminarians should have both ordinary and extraordinary confessors available to them, who should come regularly to the seminary. However, they always have the choice to approach freely any confessor, either within or outside the seminary.[169] It is fitting, for an integral formation, that the Spiritual Director could also be the regular confessor.

108. The annual retreat[170], a time of profound reflection in prolonged prayerful encounter with the Lord in an atmosphere of silence and recollection, must then be continued during the rest of the year in occasional periods of recollection and in daily prayer. In this way, the desire to dedicate his life generously to pastoral charity will gradually emerge and be strengthened in the heart of the seminarian, moulded by the action of the Holy Spirit.

109. Setting out to follow the Master with faith and freedom of heart, seminarians learn, after the example of Christ, to make a gift of their *"own will by obedience to the service of God and their fellow men"*.[171] Obedience unites us with the wisdom of God, which builds up the Church and assigns to each his place and mission. It is the duty of formators, therefore, to train seminarians in a true and mature obedience, by exercising authority with prudence, and encouraging them to give their assent, also their interior assent, in a peaceful and sincere manner.

110. The evangelical counsel of chastity develops the maturity of the person, making him able to live the reality of his own body and affectivity within the logic of gift. This virtue *"colours all human relations and leads to experiencing and showing [...] a sincere, human, fraternal and personal love, one that is capable of sacrifice, following Christ's example, a love for all and for each person"*.[172]

---

[169] Cf. *ibid.*, can. 240, § 1.
[170] Cf. *ibid.*, can. 246, § 5.
[171] *Presbyterorum Ordinis*, n. 15: *AAS* 58 (1966), 1014.
[172] *Pastores Dabo Vobis*, n. 50: *AAS* 84 (1992), 746.

As a sign of this complete dedication to God and to neighbour, the Latin Church upholds perfect continence in celibacy for the Kingdom of Heaven as especially fitting for the priesthood.[173] Rooted in Christ the Spouse, and totally consecrated to the service of the People of God in celibacy, priests *"adhere to [Christ] more easily with an undivided heart, they dedicate themselves more freely in him and through him to the service of God and men, [...] and thus they are apt to accept, in a broad sense, fatherhood in Christ [...] Therefore, those who prepare for priesthood ought to recognise and welcome celibacy as a special gift of God"*.[174] For this reason, those who are in preparation for priesthood ought to recognise and welcome celibacy as a special gift of God. With a proper emotional formation, understood as a journey towards the fulness of love, *"priestly celibacy will not be viewed so much as something that has to be given up for God as a gift received from his mercy. The one who enters upon this state of life must be aware that he is not assuming a burden but receiving, above all, a liberating grace"*.[175]

In order for celibacy to be a truly free choice, seminarians must be led to understand, by the light of faith, the evangelical power of such a gift.[176] At the same time, they should be able to esteem correctly the values of the married state: *"Marriage and celibacy are two states of authentic Christian life. Both are specific expressions of the Christian vocation"*.[177]

---

[173] Cf. *Presbyterorum Ordinis*, n. 16: *AAS* 58 (1966), 1015-1017; C.I.C., can. 247, § 1.

[174] *Presbyterorum Ordinis*, n. 16: *AAS* 58 (1966), 1015-1016.

[175] *A Guide to Formation in Priestly Celibacy*, n. 16; n. 58: "*Seminarians ought to be guided in discovering the theology of chastity, showing the relationship between the practice of this virtue and the great virtues of Christianity. The apostolic fruitfulness of consecrated virginity should be shown, noting how every experience of good or evil contributes positively or negatively to our sense of being, our personality and, consequently, also our apostolic action*".

[176] *Pastores Dabo Vobis*, n. 29: *AAS* 84 (1992), 704: "*It is especially important that the priest understand the theological motivation of the Church's law on celibacy. Inasmuch as it is a law, it expresses the Church's will, even before the will of the subject expressed by his readiness. But the will of the Church finds its ultimate motivation in the link between celibacy and sacred ordination, which configures the priest to Jesus Christ the head and spouse of the Church. The Church, as the spouse of Jesus Christ, wishes to be loved by the priest in the total and exclusive manner in which Jesus Christ her head and spouse loved her. Priestly celibacy, then, is the gift of self in and with Christ to his Church and expresses the priest's service to the Church in and with the Lord*".

[177] *A Guide to Formation in Priestly Celibacy*, n. 6.

It would be gravely imprudent to admit to the sacrament of Orders a seminarian who does not enjoy free and serene affective maturity. He must be faithful to celibate chastity through the exercise of human and priestly virtues, understood as openness to the action of grace, rather than the mere achievement of continence by will power alone.

Where seminarians of the Oriental Catholic Churches are admitted to Latin seminaries, their formation for celibacy or for marriage should respect the norms and customs of their respective Oriental Churches.[178]

111. Seminarians should cultivate the spirit of poverty in practical ways.[179] They should be formed to imitate the heart of Christ, who, *"became poor although he was rich"* (cf. *2 Cor* 8:9), in order to enrich us. They should seek to acquire the true freedom and docility of sons of God, attaining to the spiritual self-mastery that is needed for a proper relationship with the world and worldly goods.[180] In this way they assume the manner of the Apostles, who were sent out by Christ trusting in Providence, *"taking nothing for the journey"* (cf. *Mk* 6:8-9). They should have a special place in their hearts for the poorest and weakest. Already being used to sacrificing willingly and generously what is not needed, they ought to be witnesses to poverty through simplicity and austerity of life[181], so as to become sincere and credible promoters of true social justice.[182]

112. Seminarians ought to cultivate an authentic and filial devotion to the Virgin Mary[183], both through her liturgical celebrations and through popular devotions, particularly the recitation of the Holy Rosary and of the Angelus. This is because *"every aspect of priestly formation can be*

---

[178] C.C.E.O., cann. 343 and 373-375.

[179] Cf. *Presbyterorum Ordinis*, n. 17: *AAS* 58 (1966), 1017-1018; cf. also *Evangelii Gaudium*, n. 198: *AAS* 105 (2013), 1103; FRANCIS, *Address to Seminarians and Novices from Various Countries of the World on the Occasion of the Year of Faith* (6 July 2013): *Insegnamenti* I/2 (2013), 9.

[180] *Pastores Dabo Vobis*, n. 30: *AAS* 84 (1992), 706: *"Poverty alone ensures that the priest remains available to be sent wherever his work will be most useful and needed even at the cost of personal sacrifice"*.

[181] Cf. AMBROSE, *De officiis ministrorum*, II, 28: PL 16, 139-142.

[182] Cf. *Pastores Dabo Vobis*, n. 30: *AAS* 84 (1992), 705-707.

[183] Cf. C.I.C., can. 246, § 3.

referred to Mary, the human being who has responded better than any other to God's call. Mary became both the servant and the disciple of the Word to the point of conceiving, in her heart and in her flesh, the Word made man, so as to give him to mankind".[184]

The importance of an authentic devotion to the saints should not be forgotten. Among them, St Joseph, Spouse of the Blessed Virgin Mary and patron of the Universal Church, *"called by God to serve the person and mission of Jesus directly through the exercise of his fatherhood"*[185], should be placed before the seminarians and become familiar to them so that they *"will always keep before their eyes his humble, mature way of serving and of 'taking part' in the plan of salvation"*.[186]

113. Knowledge of and meditation on the Fathers of the Church should form a part of the spiritual dimension[187], since they are witnesses to the life of the People of God over two thousand years. In the Fathers *"the sense of newness of the Christian life was joined to certainty of faith. In the Christian communities of their time, this led to the emergence of an 'explosive vitality', missionary fervour and an atmosphere of love that inspired souls to heroism in daily life"*.[188]

114. Moreover, pious devotions and practices, as well as certain expressions of popular piety and religion, should be promoted and given room, especially those approved by the Magisterium.[189] In this way, future priests will acquire familiarity with the "popular spirituality" that they will be called upon to discern, guide and accept out of pastoral charity and effectiveness.[190]

---

[184] *Pastores Dabo Vobis*, n. 82: AAS 84 (1992), 802.

[185] JOHN PAUL II, Apostolic Exhortation *Redemptoris Custos* (15 August 1989), n. 8: AAS 82 (1990), 14.

[186] *Ibid.*, n. 1: AAS 82 (1990), 6.

[187] Cf. *Optatam Totius*, n. 16: AAS 58 (1966), 723-724; CONGREGATION FOR CATHOLIC EDUCATION, *Instruction on the Study of the Fathers of the Church in the Formation of Priests* (10 November 1989), n. 45. [English Translation: cf. *Origins* 19:34 (25 January 1990) 549-561].

[188] *Instruction on the Study of the Fathers of the Church in the Formation of Priests*, n. 44.

[189] Cf. CONGREGATION FOR DIVINE WORSHIP AND DISCIPLINE OF THE SACRAMENTS, *Directory on Popular Piety and the Liturgy. Principles and Directives* (17 December 2001), nn. 61-64.

[190] Cf. PAUL VI, Apostolic Exhortation *Evangelii Nuntiandi* (8 December 1975), n. 48: AAS 68 (1976), 37-38; *Evangelii Gaudium*, nn. 122-126: AAS 105 (2013), 1071-1073.

115. Over time, it is important to cultivate some specific virtues in those called to priesthood and pastoral ministry[191]: *"faithfulness, integrity, consistency, wisdom, a welcoming spirit, friendliness, goodness of heart, decisive firmness in essentials, freedom from overly subjective viewpoints, personal disinterestedness, patience, an enthusiasm for daily tasks, confidence in the value of the hidden workings of grace as manifested in the simple and the poor"*.[192] Moreover, to become truly a shepherd after the heart of Jesus, the priest *"aware of the undeserved mercy of God in his life and in the life of his brothers, he must cultivate the virtues of humility and compassion towards the People of God at large, especially those who feel themselves extraneous to the Church"*.[193]

(D) THE INTELLECTUAL DIMENSION

116. Intellectual formation is aimed at achieving for seminarians a solid competence in philosophy and theology, along with a more general educational preparation, enough to allow them to proclaim the Gospel message to the people of our own day in a way that is credible and can be understood. It seeks to enable them to enter into fruitful dialogue with the contemporary world, and to uphold the truth of the faith by the light of reason, thereby revealing its beauty.

Candidates for the priesthood must prepare themselves with diligent attention, by deepening their knowledge of the philosophical and theological sciences, with a good introduction to canon law, social sciences, and history. This preparation seeks to *"give a reason for hope"* (cf. *1 Pt* 3:15), to allow Divine Revelation to become known, and to bring all peoples to the obedience of faith (cf. *Rom* 16:26).

Reason, when open to the mystery of God and directed to him, allows a solid acceptance of Revelation, seeks a deeper understanding of its contents, and offers instruments and language for its proclamation to the world. As already stated by the Second Vatican Council, the knowledge of philosophy and theology helps us *"to hear, distinguish and interpret the many voices of our age, and to judge them in the light of the divine word,*

---

[191] Cf. C.I.C., cann. 244-245, § 1.
[192] *Pastores Dabo Vobis*, n. 26: *AAS* 84 (1992), 700.
[193] *Directory for the Ministry and Life of Priests*, n. 46.

so that revealed truth can always be more deeply penetrated, better understood and set forth to greater advantage".[194]

117. Intellectual formation is a part of the integral formation of the priest. Moreover, it serves his pastoral ministry and has an impact upon his human and spiritual formation, which draw rich nourishment from it. This means that the development of all the faculties and dimensions of the person, including the rational dimension, through the vast array of acquired knowledge, contributes to the growth of the priest as the servant and witness of the Word in the Church and in the world. Far from being confined solely to the field of knowledge or being understood solely as a means of acquiring more information in the various disciplines, intellectual formation helps priests to listen profoundly to the Word, and also to the ecclesial community, in order to learn how to read the signs of the times.

118. The organic and serious study of philosophy and theology is the most suitable means of acquiring that *forma mentis* that enables one to address the questions and challenges that are encountered in the exercise of the sacred ministry, and to interpret them in the light of faith. Yet, while it is necessary, on the one hand, not to neglect a solid and adequate intellectual formation, on the other hand, one needs to remember that the successful completion of the requirements of study cannot be the only criterion for determining the length of the formative *iter* of the candidate for the priesthood. This is because study, important thought it be, is but one aspect of integral formation in preparation for priesthood, even if it is by no means secondary. Each *Ratio Nationalis* is to expand on the essential elements outlined in this *Ratio Fundamentalis* regarding intellectual formation, taking account of the cultural and historical circumstances of each country.

(E) THE PASTORAL DIMENSION

119. Since the seminary is intended to prepare seminarians to be shepherds in the image of Christ, priestly formation must be permeated by a pastoral spirit. It will make them able to demonstrate that same compassion, generosity, love for all, especially for the poor, and zeal for the Kingdom

---

[194] *Gaudium et Spes*, n. 44: *AAS* 58 (1966), 1065.

that characterised the public ministry of the Son of God. This can be summed up as pastoral charity.

Naturally, however, a formation of a specifically pastoral character[195] must be provided. It should be such as to help the seminarian to acquire the inner freedom to live the apostolate as service, able to see the work of God in the hearts and lives of the people. Seen in this way, when he is an ordained minister, pastoral activity will take on the form of an ongoing school of evangelisation. In this time, the seminarian will begin to see himself as a group leader and to be present as a man of communion. He will do so by listening and careful discernment of situations, as well as cooperating with others and encouraging their "ministeriality". In a particular way, seminarians must be duly prepared to work together with permanent deacons and with the world of the laity, appreciating their particular contribution. It is also necessary for candidates for the ministerial priesthood to receive a suitable formation on the evangelical nature of consecrated life in its varied expressions, on the charism that is proper to it and on its canonical aspects, the better to ensure fruitful collaboration.

120. The call to be pastors of the People of God requires a formation that makes future priests experts in the art of pastoral discernment, that is to say, able to listen deeply to real situations and capable of good judgement in making choices and decisions. To make pastoral discernment effective, the evangelical style of listening must take central place. This frees the pastor from the temptation to abstraction, to self-promotion, to excessive self-assurance, and to that aloofness, that would make him a '*spiritual accountant*' instead of a '*good Samaritan*'.[196] He who sets himself to listen to God and to his brothers and sisters knows that it is the Spirit who guides the Church towards the fulness of truth (cf. *Jn* 16:13). He also

---

[195] *Pastores Dabo Vobis*, n. 58: *AAS* 84 (1992), 759-760: "*The seminary which educates must seek really and truly to initiate the candidate into the sensitivity of being a shepherd, in the conscious and mature assumption of his responsibilities, in the interior habit of evaluating problems and establishing priorities and looking for solutions on the basis of honest motivations of faith and according to the theological demands inherent in pastoral work*"; C.I.C., can. 258.

[196] Cf. *Evangelii Gaudium*, n. 33: *AAS* 105 (2013), 1034; *Amoris Laetitia*, n. 300; FRANCIS, *Homily for the Jubilee of Priests and Seminarians* (3 June 2016), *L'Osservatore Romano* 126 (4 June 2016), 8.

knows that, in keeping with the mystery of the Incarnation, this fulness of truth sprouts gradually in the real life of a human being and in the signs of history.

In this way, the pastor will learn to leave behind his preconceived certainties, and will not think of his ministry as a series of things to be done or norms to be applied, but will make his life a "place" for listening openly to God and to his brothers and sisters.[197]

In listening closely, respectfully and without prejudice, the pastor becomes able to read the lives of others without being superficial or judgemental. He enters into the heart of the person and into the contexts of life that distinguish him, above all into the internal and external obstacles that can, at times, produce problematic behaviour. He will be able to interpret with wisdom and understanding all kinds of things that condition people and influence their lives. He learns how to offer spiritual and pastoral possibilities that are attainable, and that respond to the life of the faithful and the socio-cultural context in which they are found.

The gaze of the Good Shepherd, who seeks out, walks alongside and leads his sheep, will form a serene, prudent and compassionate outlook in him. He will exercise his ministry with a disposition of serene openness and attentive accompaniment in all situations, even those that are most complex, showing the beauty and the demands of the Gospel truth, without falling into legalistic or rigorist obsessions. In this way he will know how to offer pathways of faith with little steps, that can more easily be understood and accepted. Hence he will become a sign of mercy and compassion, witnessing to the motherly face of the Church which, without diminishing the demands of the Gospel truth, avoids making millstones of them, leading rather with compassion and including all.

121. Because pastoral care is also extended to the non-practising, non-believers, and those who profess another religion, seminarians should learn how to enter into dialogue and how to proclaim the Gospel of Christ to all, aware of their deepest expectations, and with respect for their freedom. Formators, therefore, should teach future priests to create new

---

[197] ID. *Angelus* (17 July 2016): *L'Osservatore Romano* 163 (18-19 July 2016), 1: "A guest is not merely to be served, fed, looked after in every way. Most importantly he ought to be listened to [...] A guest should be welcomed as a person, with a story, his heart rich with feelings and thoughts, so that he may truly feel like he is among family".

"spaces" and new pastoral opportunities, to go out to meet those who do not fully share the Catholic faith, but who are nonetheless searching, with good will, for a comprehensive and authentic response to their deepest questions.

122. A sound pastoral formation demands not only engaging in apostolic activities, but also the study of pastoral theology. This will benefit, where necessary, from the useful contribution of the human sciences, especially of psychology, pedagogy and sociology.

123. In this effort to attain a pastoral "stature" and "footprint" for the mission, the example of priests who have preceded the candidates into the priesthood will be a great help and incentive. This will include the elderly, the pastors who lead the diocese, as well as the emeritus bishops. It is a matter of making the "pastoral tradition" of the local Church known and appreciated, the better to ease their future entry into pastoral life, for it is there that they will be incardinated and exercise the ministry.

Seminarians ought to be moved by an authentically Catholic spirit. While loving their own diocese sincerely, they ought to be open to placing themselves at the service of the Universal Church or of other particular Churches. This they should do with generosity and dedication, if it should be asked of them or if they themselves should desire it.[198]

124. According to the prudent judgement of the bishop, they should be introduced to some apostolic experiences throughout the period of formation, in the most suitable times and ways, making particular use of days or periods not scheduled for academic classes. These are indispensable for the integral formation of the candidate, and should be geared to the age of the seminarian and to the various abilities of individuals. Each seminary, in coordination with other diocesan institutions and in close contact with them, should set out what will be expected of the pastoral placement, arranging it over the year in such a way that it does not clash with the other demands of formation. Much attention should be given to the settings in which the seminarians will carry out their pastoral placements. In particular, *"when it comes to choosing places and services*

---

[198] Cf. *Evangelii Gaudium*, n. 273: *AAS* 105 (2013), 1130.

in which candidates can obtain their pastoral experience, the parish should be given particular importance for it is a living cell of local and specialised pastoral work in which they will find themselves faced with the kind of problems they will meet in their future ministry".[199]

Special attention must also be given to preparing seminarians for the particular requirements and methods of pastoral accompaniment for children, young people, the sick, the elderly, the disabled, those who live in situations of isolation or poverty[200], perhaps by virtue of being migrants[201], and for prisoners. The fundamental area of the pastoral care of families ought to receive special attention.[202]

These experiences must be guided by priests, consecrated persons or lay people who are truly expert and prudent. They should assign a specific duty to each seminarian and train him in how to undertake it concretely. They should be present, if possible, while the seminarian is engaged in his task, so that they are able to advise and support him appropriately and assist him in assessing the service he has carried out.

---

[199] *Pastores Dabo Vobis*, n. 58: *AAS* 84 (1992), 760.

[200] Cf. *Evangelii Gaudium*, n. 270: *AAS* 105 (2013), 1128.

[201] Cf. CONGREGATION FOR CATHOLIC EDUCATION, *The Pastoral Care of Migrants in the Formation of Priests* (25 January 1986).

[202] Cf. CONGREGATION FOR CATHOLIC EDUCATION, *Directives on the Formation of Seminarians Concerning Problems Related to Marriage and the Family* (19 March 1995). [English Translation: *Origins* 25:10 (10 August 1995), 161-167].

VI. THE AGENTS OF FORMATION

125. The principal agent of priestly formation is the Most Holy Trinity, who shapes every seminarian according to the plan of the Father, both through the presence of Christ in his word, in the sacraments and in the brothers and sisters of the community, and through the many actions of the Holy Spirit.[203] In the formation of those whom Christ calls and in vocational discernment, the primacy of the working of the Holy Spirit calls for a reciprocal listening and cooperation between the members of the ecclesial community, priests, deacons, consecrated persons and laity.

126. The one and only Catholic Church subsists in the particular Churches.[204] Even if formation for priesthood will normally take place in the context of a diocese, or in the institutions to which the candidate belongs, the priestly ministry is open to the universality of the Church[205] and, thus, carries within it an openness to the more pressing needs of other dioceses.

However, reference to the local Church to which one belongs constitutes the indispensable context of formation. The local Church is at the same time both the place in which the rules of vocational discernment are applied, and the witness to the progress made by each seminarian towards the human and Christian maturity required for priestly ordination.

127. The members of the diocesan community to which the candidate belongs share responsibility for priestly formation at different levels, and according to different ways and competencies: the bishop, as the pastor responsible for the diocesan community; the presbyterate, as the place of fraternal communion in the exercise of the ordained ministry; the community of seminary formators, who provide spiritual and pedagogical formation; the professors, who provide the intellectual support that makes integral formation possible; the administrative personnel, the professionals and the specialists, who contribute their own witness of faith and life, and

---

[203] Cf. *Pastores Dabo Vobis*, n. 65: *AAS* 84 (1992), 770-772.

[204] C.I.C., can. 368: "*Particular churches, in which and from which the one and only Catholic Church exists, are first of all dioceses...*".

[205] Cf. *Pastores Dabo Vobis*, n. 18: *AAS* 84 (1992), 684-686.

their expertise; and, finally, the seminarians themselves, as protagonists of the process of reaching integral maturity, along with their families, their home parish, as well as associations, movements or other ecclesial institutions.

(A) THE DIOCESAN BISHOP

128. It is the bishop who is primarily responsible for admission to the seminary and formation for the priesthood.[206] This responsibility is expressed in the choice of Rector and of the members of the community of formators[207], in the preparation and approval of the statutes, the Programme of Formation and the Rule of Life.[208]

The bishop should know how to establish a trustful dialogue with seminarians, so as to enable them to be sincere and open. Indeed, *"the diocesan bishop or, for an interdiocesan seminary, the bishops involved are to visit the seminary frequently, to watch over the formation of their own students as well as the philosophical and theological instruction taught in the seminary, and to keep themselves informed about the vocation, character, piety, and progress of the students, especially with a view to the conferral of sacred ordination"*.[209] The bishop must be diligently attentive not to exercise his authority in such a way as to undermine the Rector and the other formators in the discernment of the vocations of the candidates and their adequate preparation. Rather, he *"should maintain frequent personal contact with those in charge of the seminary, placing his trust in them, so as to encourage them in their task and to foster among them a spirit of full harmony, communion and cooperation"*.[210] One should always keep in mind that, for the good of the Church, pastoral charity, at all levels of responsibility, is not manifested by admitting whomsoever to the seminary, but by offering well-thought-out vocational guidance and a sound process of formation.

---

[206] Cf. *ibid.*, n. 65: *AAS* 84 (1992), 770-772; cf. also *Directives on the Preparation of Seminary Formators*, n. 1: *Enchiridion Vaticanum* 13 (1996), 3151-3152; *Apostolorum successores*, n. 88: *Enchiridion Vaticanum* 22 (2006), 1774-1776.

[207] Cf. C.I.C., can. 239.

[208] Cf. *ibid.*, cann. 242-243.

[209] *Ibid.*, can. 259, § 2.

[210] *Apostolorum Successores*, n. 89: *Enchiridion Vaticanum* 22 (2006), 1780.

In the case of interdiocesan seminaries, or where seminarians of one diocese are sent to the seminary of another particular Church[211], the dialogue between the bishops concerned, mutual agreements on the methodology to be adopted for formation, and the trust placed in those in charge of the seminary are the necessary requirements for a successful outcome in the formative endeavour.

Since the liturgy at which the bishop presides in his cathedral manifests the mystery of the Church and gives expression to the unity of the People of God[212], it will be fitting for seminarians to take part in it, in the more important moments of the liturgical year and of the life of the diocese, taking account of the demands of seminary formation.

(B) THE PRESBYTERATE

129. The clergy of the particular Church should be in communion and in full harmony with the diocesan bishop, sharing his concern for the formation of candidates through prayer, sincere affection, support, and visits to the seminary. Each priest must be aware of his own responsibility regarding the formation of seminarians. In particular pastors [*parochi*], and in general every priest who receives a seminarian for a pastoral placement, ought to work generously with the community of seminary formators, by open and concrete dialogue. The concrete forms of cooperation between priests and the seminary can vary, according to the various stages of the process of formation.

(C) THE SEMINARIANS

130. Each seminarian is the protagonist of his own formation, as has already been mentioned, and is called to a journey of ongoing growth in the human, spiritual, intellectual and pastoral areas, taking into account his own personal and family background. Seminarians are likewise responsible for establishing and maintaining a climate of formation that is consistent with the values of the Gospel.

---

[211] Cf. C.I.C., can. 237.

[212] Cf. CONGREGATION FOR DIVINE WORSHIP, *Caerimoniale Episcoporum*, Typical Edition, 1984, nn. 11-13, promulgated by decree *Recognitis ex Decreto*, of 14 September 1984: *AAS* 76 (1984), 1086-1087.

131. Seminarians are bound, both individually and as a group, to demonstrate - and not only in their external behaviour - that they have internalised an authentically priestly way of life, in humility and in service of their brothers. This is a sign of a mature choice to give themselves to following Christ in a special way.[213]

(D) THE COMMUNITY OF FORMATORS

132. The community of formators is made up of priests who are chosen for it and well prepared[214], commissioned to work in the delicate mission of priestly formation. It is necessary that there are formators assigned exclusively to this task, so that they can dedicate themselves completely to it. Thus, they should live in the seminary. The community of formators ought to meet regularly with the Rector to pray, to plan the life of the seminary and to assess periodically the growth of the seminarians.

The group of formators is not merely an institutional necessity but, above all, it is a genuine educating community that offers a coherent and eloquent witness to the values that belong to priestly ministry. Edified and encouraged by such an example, the seminarians will welcome, with docility and conviction, the proposals made to them for their formation.

133. According to the *Code of Canon Law*[215], the minimum community of formators for every seminary must be comprised of a Rector and a Spiritual Director. However, the number of formators must necessarily be sufficient for, and proportionate to, the number of seminarians, which can comprise more than one Spiritual Director, a Vice-Rector, a Financial Administrator, and other formators, who coordinate the different dimensions of formation when circumstances require it.

---

[213] Cf. BENEDICT XVI, *Homily for the Ordination to the Priesthood of Fifteen Deacons of the Diocese of Rome* (7 May 2006): *Insegnamenti* II/1 (2006), 550-555.

[214] Cf. *Directives on the Preparation of Seminary Formators*, n. 1: *Enchiridion Vaticanum* 13 (1996), 3151-3152.

[215] Cf. C.I.C., can. 239.

134. The Rector[216] is to be a priest distinguished by prudence, wisdom and balance, someone highly competent[217], who coordinates the educational endeavour in the governance of the seminary.[218] With fraternal charity, he will establish a profound and loyal cooperation with the other formators. He is the legal representative of the seminary, both ecclesiastically and civilly.[219] In communion with the formator responsible for each stage of formation and with the Spiritual Director, the Rector will see to it that the means necessary for discerning and maturing a vocation are made available.

135. The Vice-Rector must be suitable for the work of formation. He is called to assist the Rector, with due discretion, in the service of formation, and to substitute for him in the case of absence. In general, the Vice-Rector *"must demonstrate strong pedagogical abilities, a joyous love of his service and a spirit of collaboration"*.[220]

136. The bishop shall take care to choose competent and experienced priests for the work of spiritual direction, which is one of the privileged ways of accompanying each seminarian in discerning his vocation. The Spiritual Director, or Spiritual Father, must be a true master of the interior life and of prayer, one who helps the seminarian to welcome the divine calling and to develop a free and generous response.

Upon the Spiritual Director *"falls the responsibility for the spiritual journey of the seminarians in the internal forum, and for leading and coordinating the various pious exercises and the liturgical life of the seminary"*.[221] Where there is more than one Spiritual Director in a seminary, one of them shall be the "coordinator of spiritual formation". He will oversee the liturgical life; coordinate the activities of the other

---

[216] Cf. *Directives on the Preparation of Formators in Seminaries*, n. 43: *Enchiridion Vaticanum* 13 (1996), 3224-3226.

[217] Cf. *ibid.*, n. 60: *Enchiridion Vaticanum* 13 (1996), 3252-3253.

[218] Cf. C.I.C., can. 260.

[219] Cf. *ibid.*, can. 238, § 2.

[220] *Directives on the Preparation of Formators in Seminaries*, n. 45: *Enchiridion Vaticanum* 13 (1996), 3228.

[221] *Ibid.*, n. 44: *Enchiridion Vaticanum* 13 (1996), 3227.

Spiritual Directors and of any external confessors[222]; set out the programme of annual retreats and monthly recollection, as well as the celebrations of the liturgical year. Along with the Rector, he will encourage the ongoing formation of the Spiritual Directors.

137. Where circumstances require it, one of the formators will be tasked with being the "coordinator of human formation". He should work in cooperation with other competent persons (in psychology, sports, medicine, etc.), to establish a community environment conducive to the growth of the seminarians in human maturity.

When the seminary provides the course of studies, one of the formators is to be the "coordinator of intellectual formation". He is responsible for preparing the programme of studies approved by the competent ecclesiastical authority. He must also accompany and support the professors, with particular attention to their academic training, their fidelity to the Magisterium and their periodic professional development. Additionally, he is to coordinate the academic administrative office and is responsible for the library.

When the seminarians undertake their studies in a University or Faculty, the "coordinator of intellectual formation" is to take an interest in and follow their progress. He should assess the intellectual integration of the materials that have been studied, and prepare a complementary formative programme, regarding those aspects not addressed in the University or the Faculty.

Among the formators, the "coordinator of pastoral formation" takes care of theoretical and practical pastoral formation. He identifies suitable locations for pastoral placements, and he organises apostolic experiences in dialogue with priests, religious and laity.

138. The Financial Administrator[223], in the discharge of the administrative aspects of his office, exercises a truly formative role within the seminary community. He ought to be aware of the impact that surroundings can have on the seminarian in formation, and the value expressed by honest

---

[222] Cf. C.I.C., can. 240, §1.
[223] Cf. *Directives on the Preparation of Formators in Seminaries*, n. 45: *Enchiridion Vaticanum* 13 (1996), 3228.

use of material goods as the Gospel teaches. This will help the seminarian to acquire the spirit of priestly poverty.

139. The community of formators operates within the wider context of the "formative community", and should keep this in mind when carrying out its mission. By "formative community" is meant all those who are involved in priestly formation: the bishop, formators, professors, administrative personnel, employees, families, parishes, consecrated persons, specialists, and above all the seminarians themselves, of course, since formation will suffer without their full cooperation.[224] All of these individuals should be aware of the educational function they have and the importance of the integrity of their lives.

(E) THE PROFESSORS

140. Seminary professors are to be appointed by the bishop or, in the case of interdiocesan seminaries, by the bishops concerned, having consulted the Rector and the professors, if this is deemed appropriate. Due to the formative responsibility that it brings with it[225], this task requires a specific mandate. Professors and seminarians are called to adhere with complete fidelity to the Word of God, committed to writing in the Scriptures, handed on in Tradition, and authentically interpreted by the Magisterium. They are to acquire a living sense of the tradition from the works of the Fathers and Doctors of the Church, whom the Church holds in high esteem.

141. The intellectual formation of the candidates is the responsibility of the Rector and of the community of formators. With the participation of the "coordinator of intellectual formation", the formators shall ensure the cooperation of the professors and other experts, and shall meet regularly with them, in order to address teaching-related matters, so as to promote more effectively the integral formation of the seminarians. The professors should concern themselves with the progress of seminarians in their studies. The commitment of seminarians to their personal academic work, in all the subjects to be studied, must be considered a criterion of vocational discernment, and a condition for their progressive growth in fidelity to their future ministerial endeavour.

---

[224] Cf. C.I.C., can. 233, § 1.
[225] Cf. *Pastores Dabo Vobis*, n. 67: *AAS* 84 (1992), 774-775.

142. In the fulfilment of their specific tasks, the professors should be regarded as a part of a single teaching community[226], and true educators.[227] They ought to guide seminarians towards that unity of knowledge that finds its fulfilment in Christ, the Way, the Truth and the Life.[228]

The synthesis of knowledge required of the seminarian embraces all the other areas of priestly life, and not just the academic. The professors, in sharing and taking upon themselves the Plan of Formation of the seminary, insofar as pertains to them, ought to spur on the seminarians, and help them to make progress both in the area of knowledge and scientific research and in that of the spiritual life.

143. The number of professors must be proportionate and adequate to the teaching needs and to the number of seminarians. It is preferable for the greater part of the teaching body to be composed of priests, who can also ensure a pastoral approach in their own subject, by drawing directly from their pastoral experience. This recommendation is motivated by the fact that professors do not merely communicate ideas, but contribute to the "generation" and formation of new priests.[229]

The contribution of members of Institutes of Consecrated Life and Societies of Apostolic Life, and also of the lay faithful, can be of value in certain circumstances. Through the diversity of vocations, each professor should be able to present the seminarians with a knowledge of his or her own charism, demonstrate the significance of his or her particular contribution to the life of the Church, and offer a coherent witness to the life of the Gospel.

144. Professors must have obtained the requisite academic degrees[230]: a licentiate, or its equivalent, is required as a minimum to teach philosophy and the sacred sciences; the corresponding academic degree is required for

---

[226] Cf. *ibid.*, n. 67: AAS 84 (1992), 774-775.

[227] Cf. *Directives on the Preparation of Formators in Seminaries*, n. 45: Enchiridion Vaticanum 13 (1996), 3229-3232.

[228] Cf. *ibid.*

[229] Cf. *Optatam Totius*, n. 5: AAS 58 (1966), 716-717; *Directives on the Preparation of Formators in Seminaries*, n. 27: Enchiridion Vaticanum 13 (1996), 3196-3197.

[230] Cf. C.I.C., can. 253, § 1.

other disciplines. Professors should be experienced and have the ability to teach, and are expected to have sufficient knowledge of the disciplines related to those that they teach.[231]

(F) SPECIALISTS

145. It is possible to call various specialists to provide assistance, for example in the field of medicine, pedagogy, art, ecology, administration and in the use of social communications.

146. During formation for the priesthood, the presence and contribution of experts in certain disciplines is helpful, owing to their professional abilities and for the support they can give, where particular situations call for it. In the selection of specialists, other than their human qualities and competence in their field, their faith must also be taken into account.[232] The seminarians must sense and look upon their presence not as an imposition, but as a valuable and professional assistance for their needs. Every specialist is to limit himself to his own field of competence, without making judgements as to the suitability of the seminarians for priesthood.

147. In the field of psychology, this contribution is valuable both for the formators and for the seminarians principally in two areas: in the assessment of personality, expressing an opinion as to the psychological health of the candidate; and in therapeutic accompaniment, in order to shed light on any problems that may emerge and to assist in growth in human maturity.[233] Some norms to be kept in mind in the use of this science will be set out in Chapter VIII.

(G) THE FAMILY, THE PARISH AND OTHER ECCLESIAL COMMUNITIES

148. The vocation usually grows within the context of a community, in which the seminarian has had a significant experience of faith. For this reason, initial priestly formation must keep this influence in mind. Both the

---

[231] Cf. *Directives on the Preparation of Formators in Seminaries*, n. 62: *Enchiridion Vaticanum* 13 (1996), 3256.

[232] Cf. *ibid.*, n. 64: *Enchiridion Vaticanum* 13 (1996), 3258.

[233] Cf. *Guidelines for the Use of Psychology in the Admission and Formation of Candidates for the Priesthood*: *Enchiridion Vaticanum* 25 (2011), 1239-1289.

family and the parish of origin, or the parish to which he belongs, as well as other ecclesial communities[234], contribute significantly to sustaining and nourishing the vocation of those called to the priesthood. This is as true during the period of formation as it is during the life of the priest.[235]

Indeed, *"Family bonds are essential for reinforcing healthy self-esteem. It is important for families to be part of the seminary process and priestly life, since they help to reaffirm these and to keep them well grounded in reality"*.[236]

At the same time, from the outset, the journey of formation must elicit the inner freedom, that allows a proper autonomy in the exercise of the ministry, and a healthy distance from any expectations that the family may have, for the call of the Master requires us to *"place the hand to the plough without looking back"*. (cf. *Lk* 9:62).

149. The seminary is called not only to undertake an educational enterprise with the seminarians, but also a true pastoral engagement with their families. seminarians should know how to recognise and accept their own family situations realistically and with human and Christian maturity. They must also know how to deal with problems that may arise and, wherever possible, how to share with the family their own vocational path. The pastoral engagement of the seminary with the families of seminarians ought to contribute to their Christian development. It should also help them to accept the vocation to the priesthood of one of their members as a blessing, to be valued and supported all through life.

(H) CONSECRATED LIFE AND LAITY IN FORMATION

150. The presence of the laity and of consecrated persons in the seminary is an important point of reference in the formative journey of the candidates. Seminarians should be formed in a proper appreciation of the various charisms to be found in the diocesan community. The priest, in fact, is called to foster a diversity of charisms within the Church. Consecrated

---

[234] Cf. CONGREGATION FOR THE DOCTRINE OF THE FAITH, Letter *Iuvenescit Ecclesia* to the Bishops of the Catholic Church Regarding the Relationship Between Hierarchical and Charismatic Gifts in the Life and Mission of the Church (15 May 2016): *L'Osservatore Romano* 135 (15 June 2016), 1, 4-5; *ibid.* 136 (16 June 2016), 7.

[235] Cf. *Pastores Dabo Vobis*, n. 68: *AAS* 84 (1992), 775-778.

[236] *Amoris Laetitia*, n. 203.

life is an eloquent and attractive sign of the radical nature of the Gospel and of availability for service. For their part, the lay faithful cooperate in the evangelising mission of Christ, and offer an edifying witness to consistency and to life choices according to the Gospel.[237]

151. The presence of women in the seminary journey of formation has its own formative significance. They can be found as specialists, on the teaching staff, within the apostolate, within families, and in service to the community. Their presence also helps to instil a recognition of how men and women complement one another. Often, women are numerically greater among those whom the priest will serve, and with whom he will work in the pastoral ministry. They offer an edifying example of humility, generosity and selfless service.[238]

(I) ONGOING FORMATION
FOR ALL AGENTS OF FORMATION

152. The task of the agents of formation can be defined as interior openness, rooted in an intense spiritual experience. It is aimed at constant discernment, which allows one to learn from life and from different circumstances, and to discover in them the providential actions of God in his own Christian or priestly journey. The quality of the service rendered to seminarians can be measured from the depth of this openness, and, at the same time, a calm formative atmosphere in the seminary depends on it.

While carrying out that mission, the formator has an opportunity for growth, and can discover the specific charism of vocational accompaniment and of priestly life as a call that belongs to him personally. In this way, the seminary can become a school that prepares those who will be responsible for ongoing formation. That is to say, he who has been a seminary formator acquires a particular sensitivity and a rich experience to be able, later, to assist in the ongoing formation of the clergy.[239]

---

[237] *Ibid.*, n. 162: "*Those called to virginity can encounter in some marriages a clear sign of God's generous and steadfast fidelity to his covenant, and this can move them to a more concrete and generous availability to others*".

[238] Cf. *Pastores Dabo Vobis*, n. 66: *AAS* 84 (1992), 772-774; JOHN PAUL II, Post-Synodal Apostolic Exhortation *Christifideles Laici* (30 December 1988), nn. 49 and 51: *AAS* 81 (1989), 487-489 and 491-496.

[239] Cf. *Pastores Dabo Vobis*, nn. 70-81: *AAS* 84 (1992), 778-800.

VII. THE ORGANISATION OF STUDIES

153. "*The intellectual formation of candidates for the priesthood finds its specific justification in the very nature of the ordained ministry, and the challenge of the 'new evangelization' to which our Lord is calling the Church*".[240] To ensure the adequate intellectual formation of future priests, all disciplines must be taught in such a way as to make their intimate connection stand out clearly, avoiding fragmentation. It is to be a unified, integral journey[241], in which each subject is an important "tile in the mosaic" for presenting the mystery of Christ and the Church, and for allowing an authentic Christian vision of man and the world to mature.

"*The present situation is heavily marked by religious indifference, by a widespread mistrust regarding the real capacity of reason to reach objective and universal truth, and by fresh problems and questions brought up by scientific and technological discoveries. It strongly demands a high level of intellectual formation, such as will enable priests to proclaim, in a context like this, the changeless Gospel of Christ and to make it credible to the legitimate demands of human reason. Moreover, there is the present phenomenon of pluralism, which is very marked in the field not only of human society but also of the community of the Church herself. It demands special attention to critical discernment: it is a further reason showing the need for an extremely rigorous intellectual formation*".[242]

154. The different disciplines that make up the general programme of studies will be presented below. The *Ratio Nationalis* must contain an overall presentation of the subjects to be covered in intellectual formation at each stage of formation. It must briefly indicate the objectives of each discipline, its place within the context of the entire course of studies, the syllabus, as well as the arrangement of years and semesters, including the number of credits for each course.

The study of propaedeutic materials should last at least one year. The study of philosophy must be for a minimum duration of two years, or a

---

[240] *Pastores Dabo Vobis*, n. 51: *AAS* 84 (1992), 748.
[241] Cf. C.I.C., can. 254, § 1.
[242] *Pastores Dabo Vobis*, n. 51: *AAS* 84 (1992), 749.

corresponding number of semester hours, according to the academic system followed in some countries. The study of theology must last for at least four years (or a corresponding number of semester hours). In this way, the study of philosophy and theology must last for at least six years in total[243] (or, according to other programmes of study, which should include the quantity of academic material that ordinarily would be covered in six years).

The materials set out below for propaedeutic, philosophical and theological studies, along with "ministerial" materials, constitute the essential structure of studies in seminaries and in all houses of formation. They can be expanded or adapted by the Conferences of Bishops, taking into account their formation tradition and specific pastoral needs.

(A) THE STUDY OF PROPAEDEUTIC MATERIALS

155. Although the propaedeutic stage is prior to, and prepares for, the study of philosophy and theology, it emphasises not only the intellectual aspect, *"but also, and above all, the human and the spiritual"*[244]; *"in particular, it is important to achieve a proper balance between the human-spiritual and educational components, so as to avoid multiplying the study materials unnecessarily, to the detriment of properly religious and priestly formation"*.[245]

156. Regarding the materials to be addressed in the propaedeutic period, the situation of the particular Church and society in which the education is to take place must be taken into account. It will be necessary to be assured of the soundness of essential elements of intellectual formation, for these will contribute to the subsequent formative journey.

Care should be taken to ensure a *"sufficiently broad knowledge of the doctrine of the faith"*[246] and of those elements that pertain to an understanding of the priestly ministry. In addition, after the conclusion of their secondary studies, steps should be taken to remedy any lacunae noticed in the candidates for the priesthood concerning areas that they will need.

---

[243] Cf. C.I.C., can. 250.
[244] *The Propaedeutic Period*, III, n. 1.
[245] *Ibid.*, III, n. 6.
[246] *Pastores Dabo Vobis*, n. 62: AAS 84 (1992), 767.

157. The following is a list, by way of example, of the materials that might be included in propaedeutic studies:

a. An introduction to the reading of Sacred Scripture, allowing an initial familiarity with the Bible in its various parts;

b. An introduction to the mystery of Christ[247] and of the Church, to the theology of the priesthood and to the liturgy, through the study of the *Catechism of the Catholic Church* and of the liturgical books;

c. An introduction to the documents of the Second Vatican Council and of the Magisterium of the Church, especially the papal Magisterium;

d. Elements of priestly spirituality, with particular attention to the principal "schools" of spirituality, and to the saints who have offered the witness of an exemplary priestly life;

e. Elements of the history of the Universal Church and the local Church, especially in its missionary aspects;

f. The lives of the saints and those beatified from the diocese or the region;

g. Elements of human culture, through an acquaintance with the works of national authors, and of the non-Christian religions of the country or the region;

h. Elements of psychology that might help the self-knowledge of the seminarians.

(B) PHILOSOPHICAL STUDIES

158. The study of philosophy "*leads to a deeper understanding and interpretation of the person, and of the person's freedom and relationships with the world and with God. A proper philosophical training is vital, not*

---

[247] Cf. *The Propaedeudic Period*, III, n. 2. In general, an introductory course on the mystery of Christ that will allow the seminarians to appreciate the reason for ecclesiastical studies, their structure, and their pastoral ends. At the same time, along with the attentive reading of the Word of God, it also seeks to help the seminarians to acquire a solid foundation for their faith, to understand their priestly vocation more deeply and to embrace it with greater maturity.

only because of the links between the great philosophical questions and the mysteries of salvation which are studied in theology under the guidance of the higher light of faith, but also vis-à-vis an extremely widespread cultural situation which emphasises subjectivism as a criterion and measure of truth [...] Nor must one underestimate the importance of philosophy as a guarantee of that 'certainty of truth' which is the only firm basis for a total giving of oneself to Jesus and to the Church".[248]

159. Among the materials to be studied in the area of philosophy, systematic philosophy should be given particular importance, for it leads to a sound and coherent knowledge of man, of the world and of God, providing a wide synthesis of thought and perspectives. This formation must be based on the philosophical patrimony which is perennially valid, to which the great Christian philosophers bear witness.

Contemporary philosophical speculation must also be taken into account - especially those aspects that exert a major influence in one's own country - along with the progress of modern sciences, so that seminarians can be adequately prepared for dialogue with others, by being properly aware of the salient trends in society. Seminarians must be trained for the better integration of philosophical studies by being given a specific "philosophical methodology".

160. Sufficient space must be given to metaphysics in this period of formation, since *"The sapiential characteristic of philosophy implies its 'genuinely metaphysical range, capable, that is, of transcending empirical data in order to attain something absolute, ultimate and foundational in its search for truth', even if only gradually known through the course of history"*[249], according to *"philosophy's 'original vocation': the search for truth, and its sapiential and metaphysical characteristic"*.[250] It will also be necessary to give attention to theodicy and cosmology, which provide a Christian vision of reality.

---

[248] *Pastores Dabo Vobis*, n. 52: *AAS* 84 (1992), 750.

[249] CONGREGATION FOR CATHOLIC EDUCATION, *Decree on the Reform of Ecclesiastical Studies of Philosophy* (28 January 2011), n. 4: *AAS* 104 (2012), 219; cf. also SACRED CONGREGATION FOR CATHOLIC EDUCATION, Circular Letter *on the Study of Philosophy in Seminaries* (20 January 1972), *Enchiridion Vaticanum* 4 (1971-1973), nn. 1516-1556.

[250] *Decree on the Reform of Ecclesiastical Studies of Philosophy*, n. 3: *AAS* 104 (2012), 219.

161. The "history of philosophy" must be taught diligently, so that the genesis and development of the most important themes become clear. The "history of philosophy" is designed to instil an understanding of the continuity of human reflection and thought on the absolute, on truth and on the possibility of knowing it. Philosophical studies also provide fertile soil for dialogue and encounter with non-believers.

162. Other materials to be covered in this phase of studies are philosophical anthropology, logic, aesthetics, epistemology, ethics, political philosophy and the philosophy of religion.

163. Due attention should be given to the human sciences, such as sociology, pedagogy, and psychology, in the aspects most relevant to formation for priestly ministry. This will expand within seminarians the capacity to know the human soul, in all its richness and frailty, in order to facilitate the formulation of calm and balanced judgements regarding people and situations.

164. By this course of studies, it will be possible to enkindle in seminarians "*a love of rigorously searching for the truth and of maintaining and demonstrating it, together with an honest recognition of the limits of human knowledge*", and to do so from a pastoral perspective, giving attention "*to the necessary connection between philosophy and the true problems of life*".[251]

(C) THEOLOGICAL STUDIES

165. Theological formation "*should lead the candidate for the priesthood to a complete and unified vision of the truths which God has revealed in Jesus Christ and of the Church's experience of faith. Hence the need both to know 'all' the Christian truths, without arbitrarily selecting among them, and to know them in an orderly fashion*".[252] It is therefore a fundamental and qualifying stage of the programme of intellectual formation, because "*through study, especially the study of theology, the future priest assents to the word of God, grows in his spiritual life and prepares himself to fulfil his pastoral ministry*".[253]

---

[251] *Optatam Totius*, n. 15: AAS 58 (1966), 722.

[252] *Pastores Dabo Vobis*, n. 54: AAS 84 (1992), 753.

[253] *Ibid.*, n. 51: AAS 84 (1992), 749.

166. The study of Sacred Scripture is the soul of theology[254], and it must inspire all the theological disciplines. Therefore, biblical formation should be given due importance at all levels, from *lectio* to exegesis.[255] After a suitable introduction, seminarians should given a careful introduction to accurate exegetical methods, drawing upon auxiliary sciences and special courses. They should be suitably taught by the professors about the nature and the solution of the principal hermeneutical problems. They should also be helped, in an effective way, to gain a perspective of the Sacred Scripture as a whole, and to understand deeply the salient points in the history of salvation and the characteristics of the individual books of the Bible. The professors must make sure they provide the seminarians with a theological synthesis of Divine Revelation, in conformity with the Magisterium, so as to ensure solid foundations for their spiritual life and their future preaching.

Seminarians should be provided with the opportunity to learn some elements of biblical Hebrew and Greek, through which they can engage with the original biblical texts. Special attention should also be given to a knowledge of the biblical culture and context, especially the history of the People of Israel, so as to improve the understanding of Sacred Scripture and to come to a proper relationship with the people of the Old Covenant.

167. The sacred liturgy must be considered a fundamental discipline. It should be presented in its theological, spiritual, canonical and pastoral aspects in connection with other disciplines, so that the seminarians can know how the mysteries of salvation are present and operative in the liturgical actions. Additionally, by exploring the texts and rites both of the East and of the West, the sacred liturgy must be seen as an expression of the faith and of the spiritual life of the Church. Seminarians should

---

[254] Cf. *Dei Verbum*, n. 24: *AAS* 58 (1966), 828-829.

[255] BENEDICT XVI, Post-Synodal Apostolic Exhortation *Verbum Domini*, n. 35: *AAS* 102 (2010), 714-715: "*a profound gulf is opened up between scientific exegesis and lectio divina. This can give rise to a lack of clarity in the preparation of homilies. It must also be said that this dichotomy can create confusion and a lack of stability in the intellectual formation of candidates for ecclesial ministries. In a word, 'where exegesis is not theology, Scripture cannot be the soul of theology, and conversely, where theology is not essentially the interpretation of the Church's Scripture, such a theology no longer has a foundation'. Hence we need to take a more careful look at the indications provided by the Dogmatic Constitution Dei Verbum in this regard*".

grasp the essential and unchangeable nucleus of the liturgy, as well as that which belongs instead to particular historical settings and is thus amenable to revision, nevertheless observing diligently relevant liturgical and canonical legislation.[256]

168. Dogmatic theology, including sacramental theology, should be taught in a systematic and orderly way. It should begin with the examination of biblical texts. Then the contributions of the Fathers of the Church, from both East and West, should be studied, in order to illustrate the transmission and development of the understanding of revealed truths. The historical progress of dogmas should be shown. Finally, the seminarians should learn how to penetrate more deeply into the mysteries of salvation and to grasp the connection between them by speculative investigation. Moreover, they should learn how to interpret and address life situations in the light of Revelation, how to perceive eternal truths in the changing conditions of human reality, and how to communicate them appropriately to the People of God.

The doctrine concerning the sources of theology and fundamental theology should be presented in suitable ways from the beginning of theological formation. This should include whatever pertains to the introduction to the faith, with its rational and existential foundations, in a spirit of ecumenism and in ways best suited to the circumstances of today. Historical and sociological elements that exercise a particular influence on Christian life should also be kept in mind.

169. Moral theology in all its branches must also be anchored in Sacred Scripture, to show how it belongs intrinsically to the one mystery of salvation. Likewise, moral theology will illustrate the Christian way of acting, founded on faith, hope and charity, as a response to the divine call, systematically expounding the call to holiness and freedom. The importance of virtue and the sense of sin should be illustrated, without neglecting, to this end, the most recent developments in anthropology, all the while presenting the moral life as a path which, even if demanding at times, is always directed towards the joy of Christian life.

---

[256] Cf. C.I.C., can. 838.

This moral doctrine, understood as the "law of freedom" and "life according to the Spirit", finds its completion in *spiritual theology*. This must include the study of the theology and spirituality of the priesthood, of consecrated life, through the practice of the evangelical counsels, and of the laity. Christian ethics is called to form disciples, each according to the characteristics of his own vocation, towards the path of sanctity. In this context, it will be necessary to provide a course in the *Theology of the Consecrated Life* within the curriculum of studies, so that future pastors can acquire the essential information and theological content that distinguish the consecrated life, which belongs to the life and holiness of the Church herself.

170. Pastoral theology is *"a scientific reflection on the Church as she is built up daily, by the power of the Spirit, in history [...] Pastoral theology is not just an art. Nor is it a set of exhortations, experiences and methods. It is theological in its own right, because it receives from the faith the principles and criteria for the pastoral action of the Church in history, a Church that each day 'begets' the Church herself [...] Among these principles and criteria, one that is specially important is that of the evangelical discernment of the socio-cultural and ecclesial situation in which the particular pastoral action has to be carried out"*.[257]

171. In a context of increasing human mobility, in which the entire world has become a "global village", a course in the study of missiology cannot be omitted, as a genuine formation in the universality of the Church and the promotion of its evangelising impulse, not just as *missio ad gentes*, but also as *new evangelisation*.

172. A sufficient number of lectures should be dedicated to teaching the Social Doctrine of the Church. This is because the proclamation of and witness to the Gospel, to which the priest is called, has significant implications for human society, and aims, among other things, at building up the Kingdom of God. This implies a deep knowledge of reality and a reading of human, social and political relations, which determine the lives of individuals and peoples in the light of the Gospel. In this perspective one

---

[257] *Pastores Dabo Vobis*, n. 57: *AAS* 84 (1992), 758-759.

finds important themes pertaining to the life of the People of God, treated at length by the Magisterium of the Church[258], such as the search for the common good, the values of solidarity and subsidiarity among peoples, the education of the young, work and the rights and duties connected with it, the meaning of political authority, the values of justice and peace, social support structures, and the accompaniment of those most in need.

For some time now, experts and researchers, active in different fields of study, have turned their attention to the emerging planetary crisis, which is reflected strongly in the current Magisterium regarding the *ecological question*. Protecting the environment and caring for our common home - the Earth - belong fully to the Christian outlook on man and reality. They constitute in some way the basis for a sound ecology of human relations. Hence they demand, today above all, a *"profound interior conversion. It must be said that some committed and prayerful Christians, with the excuse of realism and pragmatism, tend to ridicule expressions of concern for the environment. Others are passive; they choose not to change their habits and thus become inconsistent. So what they all need is an 'ecological conversion', whereby the effects of their encounter with Jesus Christ become evident in their relationship with the world around them. Living our vocation to be protectors of God's handiwork is essential to a life of virtue; it is not an optional or a secondary aspect of our Christian experience"*.[259] Therefore, it will be necessary for future priests to be highly sensitive to this theme and, through the requisite Magisterial and theological guidance, helped to *"acknowledge the appeal, immensity and urgency of the challenge we face"*.[260] This must then be applied to their future priestly ministry, making them promoters of an appropriate care for everything connected to the protection of creation.

---

[258] For example, cf. Leo XIII, Encyclical Letter *Rerum Novarum* (15 May 1891): *ASS* 23 (1890-1891) 641-670; John XXIII, Encyclical Letter *Mater et Magistra* (15 May 1961): *AAS* 53 (1961), 401-464; Paul VI, Encyclical Letter *Populorum Progressio* (26 March 1967): *AAS* 59 (1967), 257-299; John Paul II, Encyclical Letter *Centesimus Annus* (1 May 1991): *AAS* 83 (1991), 793-867; Benedict XVI, Encyclical Letter *Caritas in Veritate* (29 June 2009): *AAS* 101 (2009), 641-709.

[259] Francis, Encyclical Letter *Laudato Si'* (24 May 2015), n. 217: *L'Osservatore Romano* 137 (19 June 2015), 6.

[260] *Ibid.* n. 15: *L'Osservatore Romano* 137 (19 June 2015), 4.

173. By scientifically examining the historical sources, Church history must illustrate the origin and development of the Church as the People of God, which has spread through time and space. In presenting it, the development of theological doctrines and the concrete social, economic and political situations should be taken into account, as should the opinions and categories of thought that have exerted most influence, without neglecting to investigate their reciprocal interdependence and development. Finally, the wonderful encounter between divine and human action should be emphasised, giving seminarians a real sense of the Church and of Tradition. The history of the Church in their own country should receive due attention as well.

174. Canon Law should be taught setting out from a sound vision of the mystery of the Church, in the light of the teaching of the Second Vatican Council.[261] In expounding principles and norms, it must be shown how the entire canonical order and ecclesiastical discipline must respond to the saving will of God, having the salvation of souls as the *suprema lex*. For this reason, taking the words used in the promulgation of the *Code* of 1983, it can be said that the entire Law of the Church *"could be understood as a great effort to translate [...] the conciliar ecclesiology into canonical language. If, however, it is impossible to translate perfectly into canonical language the conciliar image of the Church, nevertheless, in this image there should always be found as far as possible its essential point of reference"*.[262] Canon Law places itself, therefore, at the service of the action of the Spirit in the Church, and it favours an efficacious pastoral endeavour within a right discernment of ecclesiastical situations.

It is appropriate, therefore, that during the time of initial formation the spirit and the study of Canon Law should be promoted, in such a way that priests may come to understand that the remedy for many difficult situations or "wounds" can be found within the Law of the Church, especially concerning the pastoral care of the family. This will assist them to seek *"constantly [...], the good of the Christian faithful"*.[263]

---

[261] Cf. *Optatam Totius*, n. 16: *AAS* 58 (1966), 723-724.

[262] John Paul II, Apostolic Constitution *Sacrae Disciplinae Leges* (25 January 1983): *AAS* 75 (1983), Pars II, p. XI.

[263] Francis, Apostolic Letter motu proprio *Mitis Iudex Dominus Iesus* (15 August 2015); *L'Osservatore Romano* 204 (9 September 2015), 3.

175. At the same time, other disciplines should be considered an integral part of the course of theological studies, such as ecumenism and the history of religions, especially those that are commonly found in each country. Moreover, aware that *"we also evangelise when we attempt to confront the various challenges which can arise"*[264], it is necessary to pay great attention to those to whom the faith is proclaimed and, thus, to the questions and challenges which emerge from the secular culture: the economy of exclusion, the idolatry of money, the iniquity that generates violence, the primacy of appearance over being, postmodern individualism and globalisation, as well as the reality of ethical relativism and religious indifference.[265]

(D) "MINISTERIAL" SUBJECTS

176. The knowledge of ministerial disciplines will be required, above all, for the specific demands of future pastoral ministry[266], which will be exercised in a particular context and a precise period of history. It will be the responsibility of every seminary, according to the times and means established in each *Ratio Nationalis*, to ensure that the seminarians are taught these disciplines during the course of formation. Providing these disciplines and deepening them will be a useful and essential contribution to the life and the human and spiritual growth of future priests, as well as for their ministry.

177. It will be appropriate, in particular, to study the *ars celebrandi*, to teach seminarians how to participate fruitfully in the sacred mysteries, and how to celebrate the liturgy practically, with respect for, and fidelity to, the liturgical books.

Special attention is to be given to the homily[267], since it is *"the touchstone for judging a pastor's closeness and ability to communicate to his*

---

[264] *Evangelii Gaudium*, n. 61: AAS 105 (2013), 1045.

[265] Cf. *ibid.*, nn. 52-75: *AAS* 105 (2013), 1041-1051.

[266] Cf. C.I.C., can. 256, § 1.

[267] Cf. CONGREGATION FOR DIVINE WORSHIP AND THE DISCIPLINE OF THE SACRAMENTS, *Homiletic Directory* (29 June 2014); cf. *Evangelii Gaudium*, nn. 135-144: *AAS* 105 (2013), 1076-1080; FRANCIS, Apostolic Letter *Misericordia et Misera* (20 November 2016), n. 6: *L'Osservatore Romano* 268 (21-22 November 2016), 8-9.

people".[268] The particular usefulness of such a preparation will be revealed in other areas of ministry, such as liturgical preaching and catechesis, which are ongoing duties for priests in the work of promoting the growth of the communities entrusted to them. Preparation for proclaiming the Christian message is not only "technical", since, "*a preacher has to contemplate the Word, but he also has to contemplate his people [...] He needs to be able to link the message of a biblical text to a human situation, to an experience which cries out for the light of God's Word*".[269]

178. To make the seminarians ready and prepared for the celebration of the sacrament of Reconciliation, a specific course of *initiation into the ministry of confession* will prove to be of great importance, to help them to translate the principles of moral theology in concrete cases, and to address the questions encountered in this delicate ministry with a merciful spirit.[270] In this context, in view of the pastoral care of the faithful, formation in the discernment of spirits and in spiritual direction should receive attention as an integral part of priestly ministry.

179. Since the faith of the People of God will often be expressed in forms of popular piety, which "*manifests a thirst for God which only the simple and poor can know*"[271] and is "*a 'locus theologicus' which demands our attention, especially at a time when we are looking to the new evangelization*"[272], future priests must be familiar with it and appreciate its worth and genuine meaning. In this way, seminarians will learn to distinguish what belongs to the inculturation of the Gospel and constitutes a real treasure for the Church, from "*attachments to imperfect or erroneous types of devotion which are estranged from genuine Biblical revelation*".[273] Seminarians will also have to be introduced to hagiography as a natural elaboration of this theme, with particular reference to the lives of the saints of greatest note.

---

[268] *Evangelii Gaudium*, n. 135: *AAS* 105 (2013), 1076.

[269] *Ibid.*, n. 154: *AAS* 105 (2013), 1084-1085.

[270] Cf. for example, CONGREGATION FOR THE CLERGY, *The Priest, Minister of Divine Mercy. An Aid to Confessors and Spiritual Directors* (9 March 2011).

[271] *Evangelii Nuntiandi*, n. 48: *AAS* 68 (1976), 37-38.

[272] *Evangelii Gaudium*, n. 126: *AAS* 105 (2013), 1073.

[273] *Directory on Popular Piety and the Liturgy*, n. 1.

180. In order to be better prepared for the demands of priestly ministry, seminarians must receive a careful training in the administration of goods, to be carried out according to canonical norms, soberly, with detachment and moral transparency, along with the necessary skill.[274] This will allow for a clear Gospel witness - to which the Christian people are particularly sensitive - facilitating in this way a more effective pastoral action. This formation must include the essential elements of civil law on the subject, with special attention to the duties to be carried out by all pastors [*parochi*] and to the need to engage the services of lay people.

181. Based on the concrete circumstances of where the seminarians are formed, they will have to acquire an appreciation of sacred art. The attention given specifically to this area will provide the future priests with further catechetical resources, as well as giving them a greater awareness of history and the "treasures" to be preserved, which are the patrimony of the particular Churches in which they will work. It should be remembered that a proper appreciation of art and of beauty is in itself a value, which furthermore has a clear pastoral application. In addition, the knowledge of sacred music[275] will contribute to the overall formation of seminarians, and provide them with another resource in view of evangelisation and pastoral endeavour.

182. Considering the ample attention given by the Magisterium to the theme of social communications[276], and the promising area of evangelisation found in the "new media", seminaries must develop a specific awareness in seminarians in this regard. Accordingly, it will be necessary to understand not only technical ideas and instruments, but above all to familiarise seminarians with their balanced and mature use, avoiding excessive attachment or addiction.

---

[274] Cf. FRANCIS, *Address to Rectors and Students of the Pontifical Colleges and Residences of Rome* (12 May 2014); *l.c.* 5; C.I.C., can. 282.

[275] Cf. SACRED CONGREGATION FOR RITES, Instruction *Musicam Sacram*, on Music in the Liturgy (5 March 1967): *AAS* 59 (1967), 300-320.

[276] Cf. SECOND VATICAN ECUMENICAL COUNCIL, Decree on the Media of Social Communications *Inter Mirifica* (4 December 1963): *AAS* 56 (1964), 97-138, along with the messages of the Popes for World Communications Day.

183. Finally, the teaching of languages in seminary is of perennial relevance. It is earnestly recommended that seminarians know at least one modern language, taking account of the languages spoken in the countries in which they will exercise the priestly ministry. The questions connected with migration or tourism cannot be ignored in seminary formation, and require that a sufficient linguistic competence is attained.

As well as biblical Hebrew and Greek, seminarians should be introduced to the study of Latin from the start of the course of formation, since it provides an access to the sources of the Magisterium and the history of the Church.

184. The ministerial subjects mentioned, and others judged useful or necessary for priestly ministry, should be studied by the seminarians during the journey of formation, taking into consideration their relevance for the formation programme, and in accordance with the times and methods in the *Ratio Nationalis*.

(E) SPECIALISED STUDIES

185. In addition to the institutional studies, required for the formation of every priest, the apostolate may require of some a specialised preparation. Besides the possibility of developing some specialisation for the benefit of pastoral ministry, it is important to prepare priests destined for tasks or offices that demand a more specialised preparation by means of pertinent courses or institutes of study.

In this regard, over and above specialised study of the familiar sacred sciences, other initiatives can also be envisaged, promoted by particular Churches. These may provide for specific formation in areas considered important for certain pastoral situations, and for acquiring the tools and knowledge that will be of assistance in more specific ministries. By way of example one could mention courses for the training of those who will work in Ecclesiastical Tribunals, of seminary formators, of those engaged in the field of *mass media*, of those involved in the administration of ecclesiastical goods, and in catechesis.

To that end, after gathering the necessary information and assessing the needs of the particular Church, insofar as it pertains to their responsibility, bishops will be able to choose those who, by character, virtue and capability, they consider suitable for these tasks.

(F) THE GOALS AND METHODS OF TEACHING

186. While taking into account the variety of methods, teaching must ensure the pursuit of the following goals:

a. To help the seminarian, from the great quantity of information that he receives, to draw out the essential questions, and to awaken that healthy restlessness of heart, that opens the human spirit to the search for God;

b. To achieve the unity and synthesis of intellectual formation, by means of the reciprocal harmony between biblical, theological and philosophical studies. In particular, the seminarian must be helped to order and coordinate the knowledge acquired, so as to overcome the risk that it be learned in a fragmentary way, leading to a disorganised and confused "puzzle"[277];

c. To ensure teaching that is clear and sound, that seeks to impart better knowledge of the mystery of God and his Church, the truths of faith and their hierarchy[278], man and the contemporary world;

d. To promote dialogue and engagement among seminarians, and between seminarians and their professors, through an ability to sustain logical and rational discussion;

e. To offer seminarians an historical perspective, so that they can appreciate the connection between faith and historical development, learning to express adequately the content of their philosophical and theological formation.

187. *Practical Guidelines.* Regarding teaching methods, the following should be taken into consideration:

a. In institutional courses, those who teach should present the essential content of the subject matter, giving the seminarians suggestions for their personal study and bibliography;

---

[277] Cf. *Pastores Dabo Vobis*, n. 54: *AAS* 84 (1992), 753-754.

[278] Cf. C.I.C. cann. 750. 752-754.

The Organisation of Studies

b. Professors must take care to teach Catholic doctrine, with reference especially to the richness of the Magisterium of the Church, and giving privileged attention to the pontifical Magisterium and to the Ecumenical Councils, in order to respond to the challenges of the new evangelisation and the current reality;

c. Interdisciplinary seminars should be offered, to make common study more fruitful and to promote creative collaboration between teachers and seminarians at the scientific and intellectual level;

d. Personal study under the guidance of "tutors" should be encouraged, so that the seminarians can learn a method suitable for scholarly research and, being duly supported and encouraged, they can adequately assimilate the teaching imparted to them;

e. The seminarians should be introduced to the study of various pastoral questions by a scientific method, so that they can better comprehend the intimate connection between life, piety and the knowledge attained in lectures[279];

f. Where the Conference of Bishops considers it suitable, a period of formation can be provided outside of the seminary, at times in other countries, to learn useful languages or to get to know the life of the Church rooted in a different culture.

A basic organisational structure is required for study to be truly fruitful, and a sufficient number of well-trained teachers will be a part of this.[280] A well-organised and well-run library, overseen by competent personnel, and internet access as an instrument of research and communication, is also necessary.

Seminarians are expected to give proof of the progress made in study by exams, both oral and written, and by written papers, according to the norms established by the Conferences of Bishops.

---

[279] Cf. *ibid.*, can. 254, § 2.
[280] Cf. *ibid.*, can. 253, §§ 1-2.

VIII. CRITERIA AND NORMS

(A) VARIOUS FORMS OF SEMINARY

188. It should be remembered, above all, that the seminary, more than a building, is a community of formation, wherever it is found. Therefore, bishops who consider it feasible to establish or maintain a diocesan seminary[281], having carefully assessed the circumstances relating to the ecclesial situation, should take into consideration the need for a sufficient number of vocations and formators to ensure a formative community[282], as well as the number of professors capable of offering a quality education. Naturally, they must also take into consideration the financial viability of the institution.

When circumstances do not allow for this, it is necessary to seek a suitable solution, in consultation with the other bishops of the Ecclesiastical Province or the Conference of Bishops. This may lead to entrusting seminarians to the seminary of another particular Church, or opening interdiocesan seminaries, having obtained the approval of the Congregation for the Clergy regarding both the erection of such a seminary and its statutes.[283]

Seminarians sent to pursue their studies in an institute other than their own seminary deserve particular attention. In this case, the diocesan bishop must ensure that they belong to a true community of formation. He must carefully avoid a situation in which a seminarian, or a small group of candidates, have their normal residence in a private dwelling, where it would be impossible to cultivate appropriately either their spiritual life or their community life.

A seminarian who lawfully resides outside the seminary is to be entrusted by his diocesan bishop to a suitable priest, who shall diligently see to his spiritual formation and discipline.[284]

---

[281] Cf. C.I.C., can. 237, § 1.
[282] Cf. *ibid*., can. 239, § 1-2.
[283] Cf. *ibid*., can. 237, § 2.
[284] Cf. *ibid*., can. 235, § 2.

(B) ADMISSION, DISMISSAL AND DEPARTURE FROM THE SEMINARY

189. *"The Church has the right to verify the suitability of future priests, including by means of recourse to medical and psychological science"*.[285] The bishop is responsible for admissions to the seminary; with the help of the community of formators, he is to evaluate the human, moral, spiritual and intellectual qualities of the candidates, their physical and psychological health, and their right intentions.[286] In this sense, the guidelines for the use of experts in the psychological sciences must be taken into account[287], together with situations of transfer from another seminary or institute of formation[288], and the possibility of a candidate having homosexual tendencies.[289] In general, *"the initial selection of candidates in view of their admittance to seminary must be careful, since seminarians, as they continue their path towards priesthood, not infrequently consider each stage as a consequence and continuance of this first step"*.[290]

b.1. Physical Health

190. From the moment of admission to the seminary, the seminarian is obliged to show that his health is compatible with the future exercise of

---

[285] *Guidelines for the Use of Psychology in the Admission and Formation of Candidates for the Priesthood*, n. 11: *Enchiridion Vaticanum* 25 (2011), 1271-1272; C.I.C., can. 241, § 1.

[286] Cf. C.I.C., can. 241, § 1.

[287] Cf. *Guidelines for the Use of Psychology in the Admission and Formation of Candidates for the Priesthood*: *Enchiridion Vaticanum* 25 (2011), 1239-1289.

[288] Cf. CONGREGATION FOR CATHOLIC EDUCATION, *Instruction to the Episcopal Conferences on the Admission to Seminary of Candidates Coming from Other Seminaries or Religious Families* (9 October 1986 and 8 March 1996); SACRED CONGREGATION FOR CATHOLIC EDUCATION, Circular Letter, *Ci Permettiamo*, to the Pontifical Representatives Concerning the Admission of Ex-Seminarians in Other Seminaries (9 October 1986): *Enchiridion Vaticanum* 10 (1989), 694-696.

[289] Cf. ID., *Instruction Concerning the Criteria for the Discernment of Vocations with regard to Persons with Homosexual Tendencies in view of their Admission to the Seminary and to Holy Orders* (4 November 2005), n. 2: *AAS* 97 (2005), 1009-1010.

[290] CONGREGATION FOR DIVINE WORSHIP AND THE DISCIPLINE OF THE SACRAMENTS, Circular Letter *Entre las Más Delicadas* a los Exc.mos y Rev.mos Señores Obispos Diocesanos y Demás Ordinarios Canónicamente Facultados para Llamar a Las Sagradas Ordenes, Sobre los Escrutinios Acerca de la Idoneidad de los Candidados (10 November 1997), n. 7: *Notitiae* 33 (1997), 497.

the ministry, according to the pertinent norms issued by Conferences of Bishops, and included in each *Ratio Nationalis*. In particular, he must present the results of a general medical examination as a guarantee of a "healthy and robust constitution", along with any documentation concerning diseases, operations undergone, or special treatments that have been necessary in the past. Only the bishop and the Rector of the diocesan seminary may have access to the information contained in this documentation, and any disclosure thereof shall be regulated in accordance with the civil and ecclesiastical legislation in force in each country.

In this regard, one must take careful account of what has been established by the Congregation for the Doctrine of the Faith regarding the prudent and personalised evaluation of those who are affected by coeliac disease, or who suffer from alcoholism or other analogous conditions.[291] The Conferences of Bishops, bearing in mind the dispositions of the same dicastery relative to other health issues that could adversely affect the exercise of the sacred ministry, are entrusted with the preparation of norms regarding these matters.

Suitable health conditions must continue and will have to be verified throughout the whole period of formation.

b.2. Psychological Health

191. As a rule candidates will not be admitted to seminary who suffer from any pathology, be it manifest or latent (for example, schizophrenia, paranoia, bipolar disorder, paraphiliae, etc.), that could undermine the discretion of judgement of a person and, consequently, his ability to assume the obligations of the vocation and of the ministry.[292]

192. In this area, the theme of recourse to experts in the psychological sciences in the field of formation for ordained ministry, has already been addressed in the past by the Church and by the Holy See.[293] The

---

[291] Cf. CONGREGATION FOR THE DOCTRINE OF THE FAITH, Circular Letters of 19 June 1995 and 24 July 2003.

[292] Cf. by analogy with can. 1095, nn. 2-3, concerning the defect of the discretion of judgement and the incapacity to assume the essential obligations of marriage.

[293] Cf. *Monitum*, of the SACRED CONGREGATION OF THE HOLY OFFICE (15 July 1961): *AAS* 53 (1961), 571.

contribution of the psychological sciences has generally been shown to be a considerable help to formators, as they are responsible for vocational discernment. This scientific contribution allows the character and personality of the candidates to be known better, and it enables formation to be adapted more fittingly to the needs of the individual: *"It is useful for the Rector and other formators to be able to count on the co-operation of experts in the psychological sciences. Such experts [...] cannot be part of the formation team"*.[294] Given the delicacy of the task and the particular nature of formation for priestly ministry, the choice of such experts must be made carefully and prudently: *"Therefore, it must be borne in mind that these experts, as well as being distinguished for their sound human and spiritual maturity, must be inspired by an anthropology that openly shares the Christian vision about the human person, sexuality, as well as vocation to the priesthood and to celibacy. In this way, their interventions may take into account the mystery of man in his personal dialogue with God, according to the vision of the Church"*.[295]

193. In an atmosphere of mutual trust and openness, that must characterise the request for admission to seminary, the aspiring seminarian is obliged to inform the bishop and the Rector of the seminary about any past psychological problems, and any therapy received, as an element to be assessed with all the other qualities required in the candidate. In any case, it is appropriate to obtain a psychological evaluation, both at the time of admission to the seminary, and subsequently, when it seems useful to the formators.

194. It must be recalled that recourse to an expert in the psychological sciences can only proceed when the person concerned[296] has given his previous, informed and free consent[297], in writing. On the other hand,

---

[294] *Guidelines for the Use of Psychology in the Admission and Formation of Candidates for the Priesthood*, n. 6: *Enchiridion Vaticanum* 25 (2011), 1258-1260.

[295] *Ibid.*

[296] *Ibid.*, n. 12: *"If the candidate, faced with a motivated request by the formators, should refuse to undergo a psychological consultation, the formators will not force his will in any way. Instead, they will prudently proceed in the work of discernment with the knowledge they already have"*: *Enchiridion Vaticanum* 25 (2011), 1277.

[297] Cf. *ibid.*, nn. 12 and 15: *Enchiridion Vaticanum* 25 (2011), 1276-1277 and 1282-1283.

"*a candidate for the priesthood cannot impose his own personal conditions, but must accept with humility and gratitude the norms and the conditions that the Church herself places, on the part of her responsibility*".[298] To protect his privacy, "*the candidate will be able freely to approach an expert who is either chosen from among those indicated by the formators, or chosen by the candidate himself and accepted by the formators. According to the possibilities, the candidates should be guaranteed a free choice from among various experts who possess the requisites indicated*".[299]

195. Having prepared his report, and observing the civil laws in force, the expert is to communicate the results of his examination directly to the party concerned and only to those persons who have lawfully been authorised to receive this information, by reason of office: "*The expert, having carried out his evaluation, and also taking into account the indications offered him by the formators, will present them - but only with the candidate's previous written consent - with his contribution to understanding the subject's personality and the problems he is facing or must face. In accordance with his evaluation and competence, he will also indicate the foreseeable possibilities as regards the growth of the candidate's personality. Moreover, he will suggest, if necessary, forms or pathways of psychological support*".[300] Specifically, taking into account what has been said, those authorised to have knowledge of the information provided by the expert are: the bishop (of the diocese of the candidate, and the bishop responsible for the seminary, if different), the Rector (of the seminary in which formation occurs, and also of the diocesan seminary, if different), and the Spiritual Director.

196. It will be the responsibility of each Conference of Bishops to issue norms for insertion into the *Ratio Nationalis*, establishing the manner in which psychological evaluations are to be carried out. These norms shall also determine for how long documentation relating to the physical and psychological health of seminarians is to be stored, respecting the civil

---

[298] *Ibid.*, n. 11: *Enchiridion Vaticanum* 25 (2011): 1272.
[299] *Ibid.*, n. 12: *Enchiridion Vaticanum* 25 (2011), 1276.
[300] *Ibid.*, n. 15: *Enchiridion Vaticanum* 25 (2011), 1283.

laws in force in different countries. They shall also take into account the possible consequences, including criminal liability, of divulging, even involuntarily, facts contained in such documentation.

b.3. Dismissal

197. Whenever the community of formators considers it necessary to dismiss a seminarian at any moment of the journey, after having consulted the bishop, in general this decision should be given in writing and a copy appropriately kept. It should provide a prudent explanation, at least in summary form, but nevertheless sufficiently clear[301], of the circumstances that have led to the decision, along with a synthesis of the discernment carried out.

b.4. Seminarians Coming from Other Seminaries or Institutes of Formation

198. In general, whenever someone has been dismissed from or left the seminary and seeks to be readmitted to another seminary or house of formation, he must present a written request to the bishop, describing his own personal journey, and the reasons that led to his previous dismissal or departure from another institute of formation.[302] The Rector of the seminary to which the person seeks admission cannot absolve himself of the obligation to gather documentation, including psychological evaluations, concerning the time spent in another institute of formation, according to the dispositions of the Conference of Bishops.[303] In general, these are delicate situations that require further careful discernment on the part of formators and the greatest prudence, before such a person might be admitted.

---

[301] Cf. C.I.C., can. 51.

[302] *Guidelines for the Use of Psychology in the Admission and Formation of Candidates for the Priesthood*, n. 16: "*It is contrary to the norms of the Church to admit to the seminary or to the house of formation persons who have already left or,* a fortiori, *have been dismissed from other seminaries or houses of formation, without first collecting the due information from their respective bishops or major superiors, especially concerning the causes of the dismissal or departure. The previous formators have the explicit duty of furnishing exact information to the new formators*": Enchiridion Vaticanum 25 (2011), 1284; cf. can. 241, § 3.

[303] Cf. *Instruction to the Episcopal Conferences on the Admission to Seminary of Candidates Coming from Other Seminaries or Religious Families*.

(C) PERSONS WITH HOMOSEXUAL TENDENCIES

199. In relation to persons with homosexual tendencies who seek admission to seminary, or discover such a situation in the course of formation, consistent with her own Magisterium[304], *"the Church, while profoundly respecting the persons in question, cannot admit to the seminary or to holy orders those who practise homosexuality, present deep-seated homosexual tendencies or support the so-called 'gay culture'. Such persons, in fact, find themselves in a situation that gravely hinders them from relating correctly to men and women. One must in no way overlook the negative consequences that can derive from the ordination of persons with deep-seated homosexual tendencies"*.[305]

200. *"Different, however, would be the case in which one were dealing with homosexual tendencies that were only the expression of a transitory problem - for example, that of an adolescence not yet superseded. Nevertheless, such tendencies must be clearly overcome at least three years before ordination to the diaconate"*.[306]

Moreover, it must be remembered that, in a relationship of sincere dialogue and mutual trust, the seminarian is obliged to reveal to his formators - to the bishop, the Rector, the Spiritual Director and to other formators - any doubts or difficulties he may have in this regard.

In this context, *"If a candidate practises homosexuality or presents deep-seated homosexual tendencies, his spiritual director as well as his confessor have the duty to dissuade him in conscience from proceeding towards ordination"*. In any case, *"It would be gravely dishonest for a candidate to hide his own homosexuality in order to proceed, despite everything, towards ordination. Such a deceitful attitude does not correspond to the spirit of truth, loyalty and openness that must characterise the personality of him who believes he is called to serve Christ and his Church in the ministerial priesthood"*.[307]

---

[304] Cf. *Catechism of the Catholic Church*, nn. 2357-2358.

[305] *Instruction Concerning the Criteria for the Discernment of Vocations with regard to Persons with Homosexual Tendencies in view of their Admission to the Seminary and to Holy Orders*, n. 2: *AAS* 97 (2005), 1010.

[306] *Ibid.*

[307] *Ibid.*, n. 3: *AAS* 97 (2005), 1012.

201. In summary, seminarians must be reminded and, at the same time, it must not be kept from them, that *"the desire alone to become a priest is not sufficient, and there does not exist a right to receive sacred ordination. It belongs to the Church [...] to discern the suitability of him who desires to enter the seminary, to accompany him during his years of formation, and to call him to holy orders if he is judged to possess the necessary qualities"*.[308]

(D) THE PROTECTION OF MINORS AND THE ACCOMPANIMENT OF VICTIMS

202. The greatest attention must be given to the theme of the protection of minors and vulnerable adults[309], being vigilant that those who seek admission to a seminary or to a house of formation, or who are already petitioning to receive Holy Orders, have not been involved in any way with any crime or problematic behaviour in this area.

Formators must ensure that those who have had painful experiences in this area receive special and suitable accompaniment.

Specific lessons, seminars or courses on the protection of minors are to be included in the programmes of initial and ongoing formation. Adequate information must be provided in an appropriate fashion, which also gives attention to areas dealing with possible exploitation and violence, such as, for example, the trafficking of minors, child labour, and the sexual abuse of minors or vulnerable adults.

To this end, it would be appropriate and fruitful for the Conference of Bishops or the bishop responsible for the seminary to establish a dialogue with the Pontifical Commission for the Protection of Minors[310], whose specific competence is *"to propose to* [the Holy Father] *the most opportune initiatives for protecting minors and vulnerable adults, in order that we may do everything possible to ensure that crimes such as those which have occurred are no longer repeated in the Church. The Commission is to promote local responsibility in the particular Churches, uniting their efforts to those of the Congregation*

---

[308] *Ibid.*, n. 3: *AAS* 97 (2005), 1010.

[309] Cf. FRANCIS, *Letter to the Prefect of the Congregation for the Clergy* (9 June 2016).

[310] Instituted by Pope FRANCIS, with the Chirograph *Minorum Tutela Actuosa* (22 March 2014); its Statutes were promulgated on 21 April 2015.

for the Doctrine of the Faith, for the protection of all children and vulnerable adults".[311]

(E) THE SCRUTINIES

203. By way of an accurate and careful examination, the bishop "*with prudent forethought, and via scrutinies, [...] should establish that each of the candidates is suitable for Holy Orders and fully committed to living the demands of the Catholic priesthood. He should never act precipitously in such a delicate matter and, in uncertain cases, he should defer giving his approval until every shadow of doubt regarding a candidate's suitability has been dispelled*".[312]

204. The discernment of the suitability of the candidate is known as the "scrutiny". It must be undertaken at certain points, five in fact, along the *iter* of priestly formation: admission to candidacy for Orders, the ministries (of lector and acolyte), diaconate[313], and priesthood.[314] These scrutinies are not merely formal and bureaucratic acts that employ standard and generic formulae, but give the authoritative assessment concerning the vocation of a specific person and its development, by those who have been authorised to do so by virtue of their office and in the name of the Church. The scrutinies aim to verify the actual presence of the qualities and personal circumstances of a candidate regarding each of the aforementioned points of the formative *iter*. Accordingly, they must be prepared in writing and contain a motivated evaluation, positive or negative, giving reasons, concerning the journey so far completed by the candidate.

---

[311] FRANCIS, Chirograph *Minorum Tutela Actuosa* (22 March 2014). At the conclusion of its Plenary in October 2015, the Commission issued a Note regarding the work it has completed and, above all, specifying its proper ends and competencies, where we read: "*Particular areas of focus of these working groups include research into the assessment and ongoing formation of candidates to the priesthood and religious life [...] The Commission does not address individual cases, it does not exercise oversight, and is not a decision-making body*", Press Release from the Commission for the Protection of Minors (12 October 2015).

[312] *Apostolorum Successores*, n. 89: *Enchiridion Vaticanum* 22 (2006), 1778.

[313] Cf. C.I.C., can. 1051.

[314] Cf. *Entre las Más Delicadas*, n. 4: *l.c.*, 496.

205. While certain elements will have to be verified at specific points, for every scrutiny the community of formators must present to the diocesan bishop of the seminarian:

  a. The request of the candidate written in his own hand;

  b. A detailed report from the Rector (that of the seminary in which the candidate is being formed and, in the case of interdiocesan seminaries, also that of the diocesan seminary or of the Director of Vocations), including an assessment concerning the outcome of the preceding period, along with all the information considered useful for a better understanding of the situation and for the assessment by the community of formators, keeping in mind the requirements of can. 240 §2 C.I.C.;

  c. A report by the pastor [*parochus*] of the parish of origin of the candidate or of the parish where he has domicile;

  d. A report to be sought from those to whom the candidate was sent for his pastoral service; it may also be useful to have the contribution of women who know the candidate, thus including female assessment and insight.

206. Before conferring sacred ordination, it is also necessary to verify that the prescribed period of formation has been completed, that the candidate possesses the necessary human and spiritual qualities, that no impediments or irregularities are present[315], that the requisite sacraments have been received, and that the spiritual exercises have been completed as required for ordination.[316] In general, the norm of can. 1052 §1 C.I.C.

---

[315] Cf. C.I.C., cann. 1041-1042. Two circular letters of the Congregation for Catholic Education have insisted on the duty of bishops and of other Church bodies to inform candidates as soon as possible about the canonical discipline on impediments and irregularities; cf. the Circular Letter of 27 July 1992 (Prot. No. 1560/90/18), and the Circular Letter of 2 February 1999 (Prot. No. 1560/90/33).

[316] The following requirements must be completed for Sacred Ordination, both diaconal and presbyteral: the request of the candidate written in his own hand and addressed to the bishop, in which he states his awareness and freedom in receiving Orders and assuming its duties (both for diaconate and for priesthood); a retreat, lasting at least five days (cf. can. 1039 C.I.C.); making the profession of faith and taking the oath of fidelity, preferably in public, before the Ordinary of the place or his delegate, and the signing of the act.

must always be observed, on the basis of which suitability must be clearly demonstrated and reasons given or, in other words *"positive arguments give moral certainty of the suitability of the candidate"*[317], and not simply the absence of problematic situations.

As is known, the bishop has ultimate and definitive canonical responsibility for the call to Holy Orders. However, he has the moral obligation to consider with the greatest attention the final assessment of the community of formators, formulated by the Rector, who draws together the fruits of what has been experienced over the course of several years of formation. Experience has shown that when Ordinaries have not accepted the negative judgement of the community of formators, it has been the cause of great suffering in many cases, both for the candidates themselves and for the local Churches. The bishop should not give a date for diaconal ordination and should not allow the celebration of the diaconate to be prepared, before he is certain that all the necessary studies have been completed correctly, meaning that the candidate has actually passed all the exams required by the curriculum of philosophical and theological studies, including those of the fifth year.[318]

207. In particular the following must also be considered:

a. the outcome of the canonical notification in the place where the candidate has had a lengthy domicile;

b. observance of the age at which the sacrament of Orders can be received (cf. can. 1031 §1 C.I.C.);

c. respect for the interval foreseen between one ministry and another, between acolyte and diaconate, taking account of can. 1035 C.I.C. and of any further determinations by the Conference of Bishops;

d. verification of impediments (cf. can. 1042 C.I.C.: marriage; activities forbidden to clerics; being a neophyte; and a situation such as someone who has returned to the faith or religious practice, having been lapsed for many years, according to the judgement of the bishop), and for

---

[317] *Entre las Más Delicadas*, n. 2: *l.c.*, 495.
[318] Cf. C.I.C., can. 1032, § 1.

irregularities (cf. can. 1041, 2°-6° C.I.C.: the delict of apostasy, heresy or schism; attempted marriage, even only civilly; voluntary homicide or procured abortion; self-mutilation or attempted suicide; simulation of acts of the power of orders);

e. prior to conferring the presbyterate, a period in which the diaconal ministry has been exercised practically.

208. The requirements for the reception of diaconal or presbyteral ordination can be dispensed:

a. regarding age: the bishop can dispense up to one year; one must have recourse to the Congregation for Divine Worship and the Discipline of the Sacraments to dispense from more than one year[319];

b. regarding the course of formation: dispensation from the minimum period of formation to be spent in the major seminary[320] and concerning the subjects that make up the *Ordo Studiorum* belongs to the Congregation for the Clergy.[321]

209. The judgement about the suitability of a candidate to receive the transitional diaconate, with a view to priesthood, must also include one about his suitability for priestly ministry, taking can. 1030 C.I.C. into account. It is fundamental to recall that an assessment for conferral of the transitional diaconate implies potentially a judgement about suitability for priesthood; no one is to be admitted to the diaconate *ad experimentum*. There is a presumption of suitability for priesthood after diaconal ordination, but the bishop may be able to demonstrate the contrary, with clear arguments, both for prior behaviour, not considered at the time of admission to diaconate, and for behaviour which occurs afterwards, according to can. 1030 C.I.C.

---

[319] Cf. *ibid.*, can. 1031, § 4 e Congregation for Divine Worship and the Discipline of the Sacraments, Notice *è Noto* (24 July 1997): *Notitiae* 35 (1997), 281-282.

[320] Cf. C.I.C., can. 235, § 1.

[321] Cf. *Ministrorum Institutio*, art. 6: *AAS* 105 (2013), 134.

210. According to his prudent judgement, the bishop, taking into account the assessment of the formators, is to provide for the admission of the candidate to ordination or to express his refusal. It is fitting that the bishop express his decision in the form of a decree, providing at least in summary form the reasons for what he has decided.[322]

Conclusion

The Second Vatican Council proposed that priests should see in Mary the perfect model of their very existence, invoking her as "Mother of the eternal High Priest, Queen of Apostles and Protector of their own ministry", and inviting them to "love and venerate [her] with filial devotion and veneration" (*Presbyterorum Ordinis*, 18).

This new *Ratio Fundamentalis Institutionis Sacerdotalis* is given for the benefit of priests, whose life and formation are placed under the mantle of Mary, who is Mother of Mercy and Mother of Priests.

The Holy Father Francis has approved the present General Executory Decree and has ordered its publication.

Given at Rome, at the Seat of the Congregation for the Clergy, 8 December 2016, the Solemnity of the Immaculate Conception of the Blessed Virgin Mary.

Beniamino Cardinal Stella
Prefect

✠Joël Mercier
Titular Archbishop of Rota
Secretary

✠Jorge Carlos Patrón Wong
Archbishop,
Bishop emeritus of Papantla
Secretary for Seminaries

Mgr. Antonio Neri
Undersecretary

---

[322] Cf. *Entre las Más Delicadas*, Appendix III, n. 10: l.c., 498.